Creativity and Innovation

Creativity and Innovation

Harry Nyström

Professor of Marketing and Organization Theory
University of Uppsala

A Wiley-Interscience Publication

JOHN WILEY & SONS

Chichester · New York · Brisbane · Toronto

Library of Congress Cataloging in Publication Data:

Nyström, Harry, 1936–
    Creativity and innovation.
    Revised translation of Swedish work published in 1974
under title: Företagskreativitet och innovationer.
    'Wiley–Interscience.'
    Bibliography: p.
    Includes index.
    1. Industrial management. 2. Marketing management.
I. Title.

HD38.N9313 1979   658.4   78–8594

ISBN 0 471 99682 3

Typeset by Preface Ltd., Salisbury, Wiltshire.
Printed in Great Britain by Unwin Brothers Limited,
The Gresham Press, Old Woking, Surrey

To
Agneta, Jonas and Anette

Preface

This book may be read in different ways. To begin with most of the chapters may be regarded as relatively self-contained treatments of different aspects of company development, particularly in complex and changing environments. Organizational design, individual and company creativity, marketing and research and development strategies and a cognitive psychological approach to strategy formulation are the main topics dealt with in the various chapters. People with specialized interests may therefore find some chapters more interesting than others.

The main purpose of the book, however, is to develop and discuss an overall framework of company development, considering differences in how companies and individuals react to environmental conditions and formulate and implement strategies for change. The focus is on innovation (radical change) and company creativity to make possible successful innovation, but the framework itself also allows for more stable and positional types of company development.

While there is no end to the number of specialized books dealing with various aspects of company development, few attempts have been made to develop and empirically apply an overall, multidisciplinary framework for studying company development. This book, therefore, represents an early attempt to broaden the perspective and area of investigation, when dealing with this problem. This, by necessity, requires a wide approach to the literature, explorative empirical investigations and tentative conclusions, as will be apparent in our discussion of the early stages of the creative process in Chapter 4.

Consequently, as a result both of the chosen approach and the vast range of problems considered, no claim to a comprehensive review of the literature is, or could, be made. Instead the references exemplify various approaches in different areas and disciplines, which I believe are of interest in developing an overall view of the problem. In a sense they reflect more my own curiosity and eclectic state of mind when reflecting on and exploring the problem area, than overall consensus as to the scientific value of different contributions. They also reflect my view of how research should be carried out in new areas, and perhaps also my reluctance to accept conventional wisdom, without testing it against my own way of thinking.

Compared to the Swedish version published in 1974, this book is somewhat more than a translation and somewhat less than a new book. The empirical study presented in Chapter 6 represents new materials aimed at exploring the value of the framework in an important area, company strategies for research and development. Most of the other chapters have been rewritten and some new footnotes have been added, but by and large they are revisions rather than new versions of the chapters in the original book.

Prior to the publication of the Swedish book, some of the ideas were presented in various articles in *Ekonomen,* the *Swedish Journal of Economics, Marknadsvetande* and reports from the Institute of Business Administration at Uppsala University and the Department of Economics and Statistics at the Swedish University of Agricultural Sciences.

Both as a background for the overall framework and in the context of the specific study reported on in Chapter 6, a large number of interviews have been carried out with leading company executives. I would like to thank them for their generous interest in supporting the study.

A number of different versions of the chapters have been discussed at seminars at Uppsala University and at conferences arranged by the European Institute for Advanced Studies in Management, Brussels, The International Institute of Management, Berlin, INSEAD, Fontainbleu, Institute D'Administration des Enterprises, Aix en Provence and the Institutes for Business Administration at the Stockholm School of Economics and Gothenburg University.

I would like to thank those organizing and attending these seminars for the valuable interchange of ideas. Among those participating whose own ideas or comments on my work have been of particular value for my own thinking, I would like to mention Igor Ansoff, Henry Mintzberg, Andrew Pettigrew, Bo Hedberg, Sten Jönsson and Olof Erland.

Economic support for my work has been given by the Social Science Research Council of Sweden, which is gratefully acknowledged.

Last, but not least, I would like to thank Kristina Wootz and Christina Pettersson for typing the many versions of my manuscripts.

Uppsala, Sweden
May 1978

Harry Nyström

Contents

CHAPTER 1

The Need for Considering Creativity and Innovation in Company Development

1.1 Introduction

Few areas of economic debate are characterized by as much agreement as the role of innovation for economic development. As a general idea Schumpeter's (1934) emphasis on the importance of innovation for the business firm and society as a whole is seldom disputed. On the other hand there hardly exists any approach to company development which systematically deals with company creativity and innovation. Innovation, then, may be defined as radical, discontinous change (Thompson, 1969; Becker and Whisler, 1967), and creativity as the ability to devise and successfully implement such changes.

The aim of this book is to present and discuss a framework for studying company development, which makes it possible to consider both continuous adjustment and radical change. Companies which emphasize stability and continuous operation are called positional companies, and companies which stress dynamic, discontinuous development, innovative companies. This classification of companies is developed in the next chapter.

Following the present trend in the management literature a situational approach to company development is adopted. Positional companies are by definition best suited under simple and stable environmental conditions, while innovative companies are well adapted to complex and changing conditions.

The internal dynamics of the company in responding to change, and itself changing its structure and orientation to reflect and be able to initiate change in the external environment, are thus of utmost importance to company development. Deciding whether to avoid, or to invite, radical change is the major strategic issue facing a company. Regardless of whether companies realize this or not, the resolution of this issue will in the long run determine company development.

The classification of companies as more or less positional or innovative thus reflects the company's overall strategy, as well as its desirable structure to achieve its objectives. Other, more specific types of company strategy, with regard to for instance, internal organization, marketing and research and development, should be derived from and consistent with the company's overall strategy — emphasizing stability or change — if they are to contribute to its realization.

For historical reasons it is quite understandable that traditional economic theory does not consider discontinuous innovative development, and thus is not of much help in studying company creativity and innovation. When the foundations of this theory were laid down, achieving stability and efficiency in production was a main objective of most industrial firms. Technological and market conditions confronting these firms were much simpler and less diverse than today, and technological and market change less frequent and upsetting. Today, however, the marketing and technological environments of most companies are much more complex and changing, and dealing with instability a major concern.

It is surprising, however, that more recent attempts to develop a realistic economic theory of the firm do not pay much attention to company creativity and innovation. Cyert and March (1963) in their behavioural theory of the firm have recognized the problem, but do not pay sufficient attention to it. In their theory flexibility is created by 'organizational slack' — excess resources — which tends to develop during good times and diminish during bad. By decreasing competition within the company for resources, slack will make it easier to resolve conflicts and agree on action. It may also make possible innovations which, because of economic scarcity, would otherwise not take place. Whether or not this will happen, and the conditions for success, are an open question, however, in Cyert and March's analysis, which thus concentrates on one enabling condition, economic resources. From our point of view this is a too limited focus, but still an advance compared to traditional economic models of company decision making which do not at all consider innovation. Most economic models of company behaviour and business theory applications of such models concentrate on relatively stable aspects of company development, or at least are mainly applicable to such problems, as a result of their limited focus and time perspective and continuous view of company development. Within this framework companies cannot discontinuously adapt to environmental opportunities, by changing their strategy or structure.

Instead companies are assumed to modify their existing products and technologies in continuous interaction with customers, suppliers and other parties in their business environment. New products and technologies represent breaks in these relationships, which fall outside the analytical framework.

Basically this type of analysis thus assumes positional companies working in simple and stable environments. When applied to innovative companies in complex and changing environments overly concern with narrowly conceived short run efficiency and neglect of long run opportunities may easily result.

1.2 The need for a theory of company development

Consequently there is a need for a theory of company development which considers both continuous action, to improve short run efficiency, and discontinuous change, to provide better possibilities for long run development in changing environments. To achieve the first objective the company's ongoing operations are the focus of attention, while to achieve the second objective innovation is the central concern.

Although, as we shall see in the following, fragments of such a theory have begun to appear in the literature, so far the work has only been started. This applies in particular to the treatment of innovation in such a theory and to the problem of coordinating short run efficiency and long run development. The analysis of efficiency, on the other hand, is the main concern of most approaches to business administration. In this book the innovative aspects of company development will be stressed. At the same time the need to achieve a balance over time between the usually conflicting demands of short run efficiency and long run development will be considered.

Short run efficiency is facilitated by simple and stable conditions which make possible standardization, specialization and economics of scale and facilitate planning efforts to achieve these operational benefits. Successful innovation on the other hand — as we shall see in Chapter 4 in our discussion of individual and company creativity — requires and itself leads to diversity and change when generating and developing new ideas. Flexibility and diversity are needed to provide favourable conditions during the initial stages of the creative process and for exploring new areas in company problem solving. By disrupting existing methods and procedures, innovation leads to initial confusion, and a demand for flexibility, if this chaos is to be transformed into new efficient patterns of behaviour.

Efficiency and innovation are thus complementary aspects of company development, but only one can dominate at any point of time. Deciding when to emphasize one or the other and learning how to do this, and also how to successfully switch between the two basic orientations, is the main strategic problem facing innovative companies. Positional companies have the simpler problem of stressing one aspect, efficiency, and their main problem is maintaining a stable environment and preventing external changes from upsetting their internal balance.

In contrast to the economic theory of the firm, organization theory has directly tackled the problem of achieving a balance over time between stability and change in organizational development. As we shall see in Chapter 3 bureaucratic models emphasize stability and efficiency, while more recently advocated models, such as matrix organizations, stress the need for flexibility and diversity to facilitate change.

In studying company creativity and innovation, organization theory therefore is of obvious interest to us. Bureacratic organization structures may be viewed as the prototype for positional companies and matrix organizations as the prototype for innovative companies, as will be apparent from the discussion in Chapters 2 and 3.

Organizational design — choosing and implementing a suitable internal organization structure — thus is an important component of company development strategies, as emphasized in Chapter 3.

Another component of overall company strategy of central interest to us is marketing strategy, which is dealt with in Chapter 5. This refers to how companies manage their external relationships with customers and suppliers. Marketing, then, is not used in the narrow sense of product marketing, usually emphasized in the marketing literature. In this literature the central concern is with individual products, rather than overall company behaviour. This may be one of the reasons why marketing theory often seems to diminish in importance as a basis for decision making the higher in the company we look (Johansson, 1976). Overall company planning and strategic decision making, quite naturally, is usually viewed in terms of broad product and technology areas, while marketing theory focuses on the marketing of specific products.

Product differentiation or market segmentation are the main alternative marketing strategies considered in the marketing literature, as we shall see in Chapter 5. Both these strategies are essentially concerned with the marketing of established products and with marginal adjustments to take better advantage of existing patterns of demand. They are therefore best suited for positional companies. Innovative companies are more concerned with product innovation — radically new products — and developing such products are not part of either of these strategies.

To develop marketing strategies for new products we need to consider the product development process and not only market introduction and market development, which is the main concern of marketing theory. This requires that we look at the creative process itself, and how marketing strategies and other factors may influence this process. It also means that we need a new concept of marketing strategy, which is not tied to existing products and allows for changes over time in company orientation.

In Chapter 5 an attempt will be made to develop a dynamic classification of marketing strategies, which distinguishes between on the one hand open and flexible marketing strategies, suitable for innovative companies in complex and changing environments, and on the other hand closed and more restricted strategies, well adapted to positional companies in simple and stable environments.

Open and flexible marketing strategies, in accordance with our discussion of individual and company creativity in Chapter 4, should aid in the search for and development of new products, while closed and more restricted marketing strategies should provide efficient conditions for promoting established products.

At the same time this classification of marketing strategy is tied to total company market relationships, rather than isolated demand for individual products, and thus reflects the overall market orientation of companies which is our main focus of interest in studying company development.

A third component of overall company development strategies, which so far has received little attention in the business administration literature, is strategies for research and development. This refers to the organization and direction of research and development which in technology intensive, innovative companies may well be the major determinant of long run success. Most studies in this area as we shall see in Chapter 6 have been concerned with individual products, without considering overall company strategies for R and D and company variables related to success.

Since this is a new area of research, with little previous work to build on, our discussion of R and D strategies in Chapter 6 is directly based on an empirical study carried out for the purpose of this book. With regard to the aspects of company development dealt with in other chapters the empirical basis is more indirect and tentative, as is evident in the discussion of empirical indicators for positional and innovative elements of company development in Chapter 8.

Three basic dimensions of R and D strategies are considered in our approach. The first is the degree of internal or external orientation, which refers to whether companies rely on inside or outside expertise and competence in searching for and developing ideas for new products. The second is the extent of isolated or synergistic technology use, which distinguishes between searching within given technology areas for product ideas or combining technologies for this purpose. The third is fixed versus responsive organization of R and D, which is based on how open and flexible or closed and restricted the company's external information and contact network, idea and project evaluation and internal project work are.

Together these dimensions determine whether a company has an open or closed realized R and D strategy, with external orientation, synergistic technology use and responsive organization of R and D indicating an open strategy and internal orientation, isolated technology use and fixed organization of R and D indicating a closed strategy.

From our discussion of company creativity we may again, as in the case of marketing strategies, conclude that open strategies should be most suitable for innovative companies and closed strategies for positional companies. Open strategies should increase the likelihood of finding and successfully developing radically new products by broadening and enriching the area of search, while closed strategies should tend to narrow the scope and focus efforts towards improving existing products. In our data innovative companies tended to emphasize open R and D strategies, and positional companies closed R and D strategies. Open strategies also were clearly associated with greater success in developing radically new products, compared to closed strategies, which supports our general approach to studying company creativity.

To understand company creativity it is not enough, however, to study differences between innovative and positional companies, with regard to what strategies they should choose in their appropriate environments. Companies, particularly in the long run, can influence their environments and at any point of time to some extent choose between more simple and stable or more complex and changing technology areas and market segments.

We therefore need to analyse also the strategy formulation process itself, how companies develop their strategies, and why companies under similar environmental conditions may chose different strategies. It is not adequate for our purpose to assume, as in traditional economic theory, that all companies react in the same way to environmental conditions.

To do this we need to employ a cognitive, psychological approach to strategy formulation, which allows for differences between companies in how they perceive and evaluate environmental conditions. Such a subjective approach to strategy formulation, which allows for individual and company creativity, and may be compared to our discussion of these topics in Chapter 4, is presented in Chapter 7.

According to this approach companies do not merely react to environmental conditions in a stimulus – response fashion. They may also creatively construct their future environments, by envisioning and implementing new ideas. The more uncertain and changing environmental conditions are, the greater the need and opportunity is for innovative companies to find and exploit new opportunities. To them genuine uncertainty then may represent challenge and possibility, rather than a risk which should be eliminated. An open approach to experience always implies greater uncertainty as to future results, but as our discussion of the creative process in Chapter 4 shows, also greater rewards in complex and changing environments if companies can constructively deal with this uncertainty.

For positional companies, however, uncertainty is a threat to their stability, to be avoided as far as the outside environment and inside company conditions permit. This, then, calls for statistical techniques for predicting and forecasting future conditions, and company planning and control to avoid the negative effects of environmental change.

Our approach — centering on openness and flexibility as necessary but not sufficient conditions for company creativity — stresses the positive effects of uncertainty and change, in widening and enriching experience. Since both flexibility and control are necessary aspects of company development — with varying emphasis between companies and over time — our approach does not question the need for conventional approaches to company management, emphasizing company planning and control. It does, however, call for a critical appraisal of the implication of such management techniques for company development under different environmental conditions and points to the at least as pressing need for most companies today to consider also the need for company creativity and innovation.

1.3 Summary of Chapter 1

In this chapter, as an introduction to the book, the need for considering creativity and innovation in company development is discussed. A comprehensive framework of company development must make possible the study of long run discontinuous company development superposed on the continuous day-to-day running of company operations. Discontinuous change — that is sudden radical alterations in the company's activities — have been designated here as innovations, and successful innovations have been regarded as the result of company creativity.

Such an approach to company development is particularly necessary to the study of company development in complex and changing — and therefore highly uncertain — environments. And yet the economic theory of the firm — and most business administration models — are mainly concerned with the analysis of continuous marginal adjustment in company operations and therefore best suited to the analysis of established firms — what in this book are called positional companies — in simple and stable environments.

This is due to their focus on short run efficiency, which is easiest to achieve under such conditions. For analysing innovative companies in complex and changing environments we need a different framework which, while recognizing the need for operational efficiency, starts with the need for long run development.

The purpose of this book is to suggest some points of importance in developing a framework for studying both efficiency and development aspects of company development and to indicate some lines along which we may usefully proceed. Most treatments of company development stress one aspect of company strategy, such as internal organization or marketing. In the present book an attempt has been made to apply a wider approach, centering on three aspects of overall company strategy, organization, marketing and research and development.

These aspects are viewed in relation to the overall strategies of positional and innovative companies, emphasizing on the one hand stability and on the other hand change.

Open and flexible organization, marketing and R and D strategies are viewed as essential to innovative companies in finding and developing new ideas and areas of application, while positional companies may benefit directly by more closed and restricted strategies. At the same time company creativity requires being able to both widen and narrow the problem scope and area of investigation, and innovative companies therefore need flexible strategies also for the purpose of switching between these two modes of problem solving and decision making.

Finally, we also need to study the process of strategy formulation itself, if we want to be able to explain why some companies tend to become positional and other companies innovative under similar environmental conditions and why companies may vary over time in their emphasis on stability versus change. For this purpose a cognitive model of strategy formulation will be developed and discussed, which allows for differences in the ways in which companies perceive and evaluate environmental conditions.

1.4 Outline of the book

In Chapter 2, our basic model of positional and innovative companies will be presented. Following this, in Chapter 3, organization structure will be considered, in discussing the importance of organizational flexibility and diversity for company development.

Chapter 4 deals with the conditions for company creativity against the background of the requirements for individual creativity and a model of company problem solving. After this marketing strategy and company development is discussed in Chapter 5 and an empirical application of the proposed framework for studying company development to the so-far neglected area of company strategies for research and development is presented in Chapter 6. This study gives support to the overall proposition that open and flexible strategies provide favourable conditions for company creativity and innovation. In Chapter 7 our cognitive psychological model of strategy formulation is discussed and Chapter 8 is concerned with suggesting some general empirical indicators of positional and innovative elements of company development.

CHAPTER 2

Innovative and Positional Companies – a Basic Classification

2.1 Introduction

In this chapter a general classification of companies (Nyström, 1971) will be presented to serve as a basis for our continued discussion. As we shall see in Chapter 3 several attempts have been made in the organization literature to separate companies into two categories based on how well adapted they are to initiating and responding to environmental change.

The distinction between innovative and positional companies, suggested here, differs however from these other classifications by referring to more total, overall company behaviour and by considering both the structure of the company and its strategy, that is its desired future development.

Other classifications usually only consider structural differences — mainly related to organization structure — and do not deal with differences in strategy between companies. Instead they essentially assume that the structure of a company determines its strategy.

Our classification considers the existing structure of a company as an important factor in determining its development over time. But it also views the perceptions and evaluations of top managers with regard to the future of the company — in other words the company's strategic orientation — as equally important.

From our point of view classifications which merely consider structural differences between companies are of value, since they may help to explain some aspects of company development. But they are limited in not also considering strategy formulation and implementation. Complex and changing environments require open and flexible structures to permit reorientation (Norman, 1971) and radical change. Structural constraints, then, are less binding and the need for radical change is coupled with freedom in formulating and implementing strategies.

In addition our classification model is more general and basic, compared to other classification models. It deals with changes in company development without specifying what these changes refer to. The main question is whether these changes are continuous or discontinuous, that is whether they are smooth and gradual or sudden and disruptive. This makes possible a general analysis of company development in different environments requiring different development strategies. Since the economic theory of the firm, and most business administrative models, only consider continuous change our analysis may be viewed as an attempt to extend the traditional economic framework by also dealing with strategies for discontinuous change.

The generality of our basic approach, while facilitating theoretical analysis and comparisons with alternative approaches, also, of course, leads to problems in applying the framework to empirical data. This, however, is more a necessary limitation of the chosen problem area, than a deficiency which may be eliminated without invalidating the analysis. Complex problems require a wide approach, to ensure that vital aspects are not missed. This implies that the theoretical models which guide the overall analysis must not be unduly restricted by limiting their applicability to narrow classes of empirical data.

Instead — when applying the theoretical models — empirical indicators may be used to reflect as closely as possible the theoretical categories in specific cases. The generality of the basic analysis will then be retained, and what indicators are used will vary with the situations studied. In Chapter 6 an empirical application of the overall theoretical framework to the study of R and D strategies will be presented, which illustrates the use of empirical indicators of the theoretical concepts in a concrete research situation. In Chapter 8 the choice of general empirical indicators to reflect innovative and positional tendencies in company development will be discussed in a wider empirical context.

In this chapter the basic theoretical classification of companies will be presented and a dynamic model of company development outlined. The discussion assumes that company development may be viewed as a tendency to change from one basic type of company to another. Our company classification and development model assumes an ideal classification of companies which emphasizes and highlights features which in the real world are less pronounced. Actual companies will tend to be more or less innovative or positional, rather than examples of the extreme cases which are employed in the theoretical analysis to simplify the discussion and focus it on the main issues.

2.2 The basic classification model

The starting point for the basic classification of companies presented here, is the distinction between a structural and a strategic component in company development. This type of distinction (Chandler, 1962; Ansoff, 1965) is often made in the business literature, but the psychological process of strategy formulation, which is emphasized in this book, is usually not considered. Our approach stresses the importance of both strategy formulation and structural constraints for company development. Central concepts introduced for this purpose are *innovative potential* and *innovative orientation*.

Innovative potential

The quicker and more radically a company can carry out innovative change, the greater its innovative potential is at that point of time. Or, in other words, the less the structural constraints on development are. These constraints are due to existing company structures with regard to, for instance, organization, production and marketing, which together, in the short run, limit the rate of change which a company may achieve.

If we assume that a company is efficiently utilizing its resources, the prevailing structural restrictions on change will largely depend on the short run profitability the company desires. Greater openness and flexibility in organization, research and development and marketing implies a greater innovative potential, which in the long run, in a changing environment, is necessary for survival. In the short run, however, this openness and flexibility is usually undesirable from an operational point of view, since it is difficult to combine with specialization and stability. High innovative potential then, in the short run, may be expected to lead to less profit, then would be possible with a more closed and restricted, highly specialized company structure designed for existing conditions. It is the price companies have to pay for successful long run development in changing environments.

A company's innovative potential may therefore be regarded as a general *development resource*, which creates favourable conditions for company creativity and innovation. As we will see in Chapter 4, intellectual openness and flexibility are necessary, but not sufficient, conditions for individual creativity. Similarly, openness and flexibility in combining and recombining information and resources are necessary, but not sufficient conditions for company creativity. To make possible successful innovation, openness and flexibility have to be combined with the focusing of efforts in the right direction. In Chapter 4 this problem will be discussed against the background of the individual creative process and company problem solving.

This way of looking at the problem makes open and exploratory search strategies more interesting from a company development point of view in complex and changing environments, compared to long run forcasts of what will happen in the future. The long run planning literature usually emphasizes the need for formal coordination and the possibility of predicting the future (Grinyer, 1971; Back, 1973), while our approach focuses on openness and flexibility in company problem solving. Innovative change, by definition, leads to great uncertainty and an inadequate statistical basis for detailed planning and prediction. This leads to a high need for innovative potential in companies confronted by such change, to make possible a creative approach to company development.

Instead of viewing the company as a closed system which can control and stabilize its environment and thereby itself determine its future development, our approach views the company as an open system (Buckley, 1967). This means that the future development of the company is seen as limited by the restrictions built into the structure of the company, but to a large extent determined by unpredictable environmental response to company action. A basic need for this innovative system, then, is to eliminate as much as possible of the structural restrictions to achieve flexibility, without disregarding the short run need for operational efficiency. Designing the degree of innovative potential to achieve a suitable balance between development possibilities and conditions favourable to operational efficiency — between openness and closure — thus is a basic strategic problem to companies working in complex and changing environments.

Innovative orientation

The fact that a company has a large innovative potential does not, as we have noted above, ensure that innovative change will take place. Such change also requires an active component in the company, which initiates and focuses change in company action within the range of possibilities created by innovative potential. This active strategic element, *innovative orientation*, is just as essential for company development, as the passive strategic possibilities which existing innovative potential represents. The lack or existance of clear innovative orientation in company strategy, together with little or large innovative potential, are the basic categories of our company classification model.

Clear innovative orientation means that the company's leading decision makers have implicitly or explicitly realized the need for radical change in company behaviour, when devising and implementing company development strategies. In Chapter 7 innovative orientation — or lack of such orientation — will be considered in the context of a cognitive psychological model of strategy formulation. In the present chapter it is sufficient for our classification purposes to define innovative orientation in a more general way, as we have done so far. This makes it possible for us to distinguish between our main company categories, as a basis for the continued analysis.

In the economic theory of the firm the strategic problem of achieving innovative orientation does not exist. The analysis assumes, instead, that structural constraints are completely binding in determining company development. Since the structure of the company is assumed not to change over time, only marginal, continuous adjustments are possible and company development becomes a question of calculation rather than judgement. Innovative potential then represents economic waste, since openness and flexibility — which widen the area of strategic choice — no longer have any justification. Company development in economic theory is assumed to take place automatically in response to environmental change, and strategic differences between companies, with regard to how they react to future conditions, are not considered.

Naturally, this type of economic analysis is not suitable for analysing company development in highly complex, changing and uncertain environments. Such environments require discontinuous innovative change for long run success, and the analysis of such change is, by definition, not possible within a traditional economic framework.

To analyse such discontinuous change we need, instead, a different model of company problem solving and decision making. Dealing with discontinuities, demands openness and flexibility and a clear sense of direction. In other words the company needs both innovative potential and innovative orientation. How to achieve successful development under such conditions is the subject of company creativity, as we shall see in Chapter 4.

Innovative and positional companies

We are now ready to present our basic classification model (Figure 2.1). This model includes two pure categories, innovative and positional companies, and two intermediary categories, which each shows one defining characteristic of each pure form, but lacks the other.

Innovative companies are companies which have developed and retained a large innovative potential and also show a clear innovative orientation. They have both the openness and flexibility necessary to conceive of and carry out innovation and a realization of the need for such radical change.

Positional companies are companies which lack both innovative potential and clear innovative orientation. They have neither the ability to innovate, nor do they perceive any need to carry out radical change.

Companies which lack either innovative potential or orientation we will call *latent positional/innovative companies*. In one respect they resemble each type of company, and by changing in the other respect, they may become positional or innovative companies.

Hypothetically we will assume that positional and innovative companies are more stable company forms than latent positional/innovative companies, since strategy and structure are internally consistent. In the case of innovative companies they both want to and can formulate and implement radical change, while in the case of positional companies they neither can, nor want to. With regard to latent positional/innovative companies they either can, but do not want to, or want to but cannot, which shows an imbalance between ability and

Innovative orientation	Innovative potential	
	Large	Small
Clear	Innovative company	Latent positional/innovative company
Unclear	Latent positional/innovative company	Positional company

Figure 2.1. A Basic Company Classification Model

aspiration. This should tend to be destabilizing with regard to the existing organization.

On the other hand what has been said does not mean that positional and innovative companies will always remain in the same category. Either innovative potential or innovative orientation may develop or disappear over time, and companies will then change from one type to another. What it does mean is that both positional and innovative companies will tend to be more stable than latent positional/innovative companies.

One result of our cognitive psychological model of strategy formulation in Chapter 7 is that it is likely that innovative companies, if they are successful, will tend to lose their clear innovative orientation in the long run. This means that they will become, instead, latent positional/innovative companies.

Positional companies, on the other hand, will tend to maintain their basic orientation if they are successful. This means that positional companies are probably more stable over time than innovative companies, in the types of environments for which they are suited.

Latent positional/innovative companies, however, are inherently unstable in the short run, even in environments in which they are successful, according to our analysis. If they initially lack clear innovative orientation, but have a large innovative potential, they may be expected to either develop a clear innovative orientation or to lose their innovative potential. In the former case they will change from a latent positional/innovative company to a positional company, and in the latter case to an innovative company.

The most likely reason why a latent positional/innovative company may become a positional company, is that short run operational advantages are emphasized, rather than long run development aspects. Resources may, for instance, be allocated to technical rationalization, in order to achieve greater short run efficiency, instead of to research and development, in order to favour long run development. Or the organization structure may be highly specialized to closely reflect existing business requirements, rather than made more open, to accommodate change.

The reason a latent positional/innovative company may develop instead into an innovative company may be a change in top management. More creative and dynamic leaders, capable and willing to conceive of and carry out radical change, may then give the company the clear innovative orientation it was previously lacking. This is probably the most common, and often the only way, to revive a stagnant company.

Similarly a latent positional/innovative company, which initially has little innovative potential but a clear innovative orientation, may become either a innovative company or a positional company. By emphasizing research and development and organizational and marketing flexibility it may increase its innovative potential and turn into an innovative company. By focusing the attention of top management almost completely on day-to-day decision making it may, instead, lose its clear innovative orientation and because a positional company. In these instances, too, a change in top management will probably facilitate the change from a more open to a more closed type of company or vice versa. By what has been said so far it follows that companies, to develop successfully in complex and changing environments, need to be innovative during formative stages of their development process. But even in this type of environment it should be of advantage to companies to be positional during later development stages, to consolidate and reap the benefits of the position they have achieved.

This makes a cyclical pattern of changes in basic company orientation — from innovative to positional and back again to innovative — the most likely pattern of successful development for companies in complex and changing environments. In stable, simple environments, however, companies may benefit from a more constant positional orientation even in the long run. It is then possible both to achieve and maintain short run efficiency without innovative change and openness and flexibility are unnecessary for success during all stages of company development.

It is clear, therefore, that the terms innovative and positional are not by themselves good or bad in describing company development. Depending on what type of environment a company is working in, and its stage of development, either can be desirable in a particular situation. This conditional view of company development characterizes the present study, and is evident in the basic classification model.

In this section our interest has been concentrated on the basic classification scheme. The question how company development actually takes place over time, and the conditions for change from one type of company to another, have not been treated in detail. Instead the discussion in this respect has mainly been an illustration of our general approach. In Chapter 7 a more far-reaching explanation of the dynamic process of company development will be attempted, by employing a cognitive model of strategy formulation and applying this model to a specific empirical situation.

2.3 Applicability of the theoretical framework

One question with regard to the classification scheme has so far not been discussed. This is how well actual companies confirm to our theoretical categories. In practice companies, of course, will not be pure examples of the theoretical cases. These categories serve the purpose of isolating and making amenable to general theoretical analysis the essential features of real company development. When applying the theoretical analysis we need, as in the empirical application in Chapter 6 to view companies as more or less positional or innovative. We also need to consider variations within companies in how positional or innovative they are.

R and D units, for instance, should be more innovative and operational units more positional. Multiproduct firms should be more positional in parts of the organization mainly concerned with established products, and more innovative in parts concerned with new products. Ways of achieving this type of differentiation within companies are discussed in Chapter 3, when dealing with organizational problems related to company development.

2.4 Summary of Chapter 2

In this chapter I introduce a basic classification of companies as innovative, positional or latent positional/innovative. The main idea here is that different types of environments call for different qualities on the part of companies operating within their bounds — if these companies are to develop successfully.

Positional companies are those which lack both innovative potential — the ability to alter radically the direction of operations within the company — and innovative orientation — a desire on the part of management to formulate and implement strategies for change. This type of company will probably fit best into — and will help to create — a simple, uniform and stable environment.

Innovative companies, on the other hand, represent the other theoretical extreme. Companies of this kind possess great innovative potential and a clearly innovative orientation, in other words they have both the opportunity and the will to undertake radical reorientations. Companies of this kind can therefore be expected to fit into complex and changing environments, where there is relatively little chance of predicting and planning operations and where flexibility in the company structure and in the attitude of its management towards the future is therefore very important.

Apart from these two extreme cases our basic classification embraces two intermediary categories. These latent positional/innovative companies can be expected to be unstable in themselves and to tend to develop towards one or other of the extremes.

This does not mean that in practice positional and innovative companies will always represent stable forms — their innovative potential or innovative orientation may disappear for various reasons that are outside the scope of the present classification model. It simply means that these forms will tend to be stable within the framework of the model. In Chapter 7 I will suggest — basing my argument on a cognitive psychological model of strategy formulation — that for quite other reasons an innovative company is likely to be less stable in practice than a positional company, given that each company's environmental conditions are favourable to their respective requirements. In other words, there will probably be a strong tendency for positional companies in stable circumstances to maintain their positional orientation, while in the longer run innovative companies will probably show greater instability — even if the changeable and complex environmental conditions which are suitable to such companies persist.

This basic theoretical classification of company types gives us ideal categories, which help us to isolate essential factors influencing company development under different environmental conditions. Thus real life companies will not in practice represent pure examples of these theoretical cases. But they are likely to display, in varying degrees, different features of the ideal cases.

The theoretical classification can therefore be used to steer empirical studies, but it will be necessary first to construct some empirical indications of our basic concepts. When I use the concepts *positional* or *innovative* in empirical context the reader can assume that I mean that in light of the chosen empirical indicators, the particular company — or part of a company — belongs to one or the other theoretical category. In applying the concepts to empirical cases we will also have to consider how uniformly or otherwise the studied attributes do actually characterize the companies concerned. The positional or innovative elements are rarely a uniform phenomenon in companies (and indeed should not be either) and such variations will be discussed in more detail in Chapter 3 in connection with organizational design.

An example of applying the theoretical framework in an empirical study is presented in Chapter 6, dealing with company strategies for R and D. In a wider empirical context this problem is treated in Chapter 8, in our discussion of empirical indicators of positional and innovative elements of company development.

CHAPTER 3

The Importance of Organizational Flexibility and Diversity for Company Creativity and Innovation

3.1 Introduction

In this chapter we will discuss the general importance of organizational flexibility and diversity for company development. In innovative companies, organizational flexibility and diversity are desirable attributes making possible and stimulating innovative change. Positional companies, on the other hand, have little need for such flexibility and diversity, indeed they may be viewed as disturbing factors of company development in stable environments.

In Chapter 4, the importance of flexibility and diversity for company creativity will be directly considered against the background of the requirements of the individual creative process and creative company problem solving. In this chapter, we will deal with the more indirect question of how the organization structure of a company, by contributing to organizational flexibility and diversity, may affect the conditions for and realization of company creativity.

Organizational flexibility is seen here as mainly depending on the degree of formalization in the organization structure (Bell, 1967). This refers to the rules and procedures for carrying out activities and the prescribed relationships between organization members, explicitly stated in organization manuals, work instructions and other company documents (Hage and Aiken, 1970; Pugh and coworkers, 1968). These directions constrain and control the decisions and actions of individual members. They may thus be viewed as restrictions on the freedom of individual members to carry out their own ideas. The more explicit, detailed and fixed over time the instructions and prescribed relationships are, the higher the degree of formalization and the lower the organizational flexibility are. The greater the difficulties then also will be for companies to successfully formulate, respond to and implement radical change.

Our discussion of organizational flexibility thus emphasizes the role of the formal structure, but this does not mean that informal relationships are not considered. It is assumed instead that it is posssible to design the formal structure so that it supports, rather than works against, informal relationships among organization members and companies then can avoid a conflict between the two. This line of reasoning assumes that organization members basically accept and follow organizational rules and procedures, if they are well adapted to the internal and external environment of the company. A major problem facing the company in designing its organization structure then is to achieve a long run correspondence between organizational flexibility and environmental needs. The more complex and changing the environment, the greater the need for flexibility and the more simple and stable, the lesser the need.

Organizational flexibility may not only facilitate the successful implementation of radical, innovative change. It may also help to provide favourable conditions for company creativity by increasing the spontaneous interaction between organization members and activitues. This should tend to lead to organizational diversity, a broad and variegated mixture of knowledge and experience in the company, which, as we shall see in Chapter 4, is a basic requirement for individual and company creativity.

Historically, organization theory applications to business problems (Wren, 1972) have been dominated by a basically static and closed view of company development, focusing on continuous company behaviour in relatively stable company environments. Organizational flexibility and diversity have not been key issues. Nowadays, however, the attention is more directed towards open and flexible organization forms, better adapted to complex and changing environmental conditions (Burns and Stalker, 1961; Lawrence and Lorsch, 1967; Hedberg, Nyström and Starbuck, 1976).

We must not forget, however, that innovative companies have a need not only for flexibility and change, but also for concentration and stability to achieve efficiency in short run operations. Achieving a balance in the organization structure between openness and flexibility — to stimulate and carry out innovation — and closure and concentration — to achieve efficiency in short run operation — then becomes the major organizational problem of innovative companies. Positional companies, as long as environmental conditions remain simple and stable, have the easier problem of mainly restricting and concentrating the structure to promote efficiency.

In the following we will, to begin with, distinguish between two basic types of organization structures. The first, the bureaucratic model, is highly formalized and inflexible and may be expected to lead to a low level of organizational diversity, by restricting the perspectives of and interaction between organization members. The second, the matrix organization, is relatively unformalized and flexible, and should lead to greater organizational diversity, by mixing together organization members and widening their outlooks.

It follows, then, that the bureaucratic structure may be viewed as suitable for positional companies, by emphasizing the attainment of short run efficiency under simple, stable and predictable conditions. The matrix structure, on the other hand, by emphasizing the need for flexibility and diversity — and indicating how to achieve a balance between the two — should be well adapted to the needs of innovative companies.

After our discussion of the two basic models we will present and discuss a number of more specific organization structures — such as functional, product and project organizations — which are used in actual practice as more or less open and flexible structures. They, then, are more or less characterized by the features of the basic theoretical models. Finally, we will discuss two organizational classification models, distinguishing between static–dynamic and mechanistic–organic structures, which have been proposed in the organization literature to reflect differences between organizations appropriate to simple and stable or complex and changing conditions. They, thus, are of interest in connection with our basic classification of positional and innovative companies.

3.2 Bureaucratic model

As a basic model of a highly formalized and closed organization structure the *Bureaucratic Organization* will be employed. This model is based to a large extent on Weber's influential work on bureaucracy around 1900, but the main assumptions are implicit in the classical economic theory of the firm, which was founded much earlier. Bureaucratic theory has been very influential in the analysis of business organizations — and still is to a lesser extent — as well as in more general, sociological organization theory (Albrow, 1970).

Taylor's *Scientific Management* (Taylor, 1911) and Fayol's *Administrative Principles* (Fayol, 1949) are, for instance, largely derived from, and consistent with, bureaucratic theory. Even today bureaucratic concepts, such as management by hierarchy and specialization by function, are often used in organizational analysis.

What, then, are the defining characteristics of the basic bureaucratic model and related models in organization theory? Weber himself distinguishes between different types of legitimate authority — traditional, charismatic and legal — as a basis for classifying organizations. He views legal authority with bureaucratic staff as characteristic of the fully developed, bureaucratic organization which, he contends, is the most rational, or in our terminology efficient, organization structure. The most important distinguishing features of this basic bureaucratic model (Weber, 1947) are:

1. The members of the organization must obey the legally established impersonal order, which has been established as a result of routinization and institutionalization of personal, charismatic leadership.

2. Leadership is based on official status and people who are assigned to specific functions are assumed to have the necessary, specialized competence to perform well in their offices.

3. The organization of offices follows the principle of hierarchy (Figure 3.1A). This means that each lower office is under the control and supervision of a higher one. It also implies that only vertical types of communication and influence, between leaders and subordinates, are recognized in the organization structure, and not horizontal relationships, between officials with equal status.

4. Organizational activities may be clearly separated from each other and independently carried out by appropriate officials. This we may call systematic specialization by function.

5. Officials are appointed on the basis of technical qualification and are

personally free and subject to authority only only with respect to their impersonal office obligations.

6. Administrative acts, decisions and rules are formulated and recorded in writing. This puts emphasis on the explicit, formal aspects of the organization structure and, together with the other requirements of the bureaucratic model, tends to make it highly formalized in intention and operation.

If we compare this basic model with what has been said so far about company development in different environments, a number of conclusions follow. To begin with the bureaucratic model emphasizes the internal functioning of the organization, and its external environment must be relatively stable and predictable, to make possible, and organizationally desirable, the type of internal efficiency postulated. This essentially means that the organization must be able to control its external environment, for instance by creating and utilizing a monopoly situation. It is therefore, from this point of view, not surprising that government monopolies are often cited as typical examples of bureaucratic organizations.

The main function of the bureaucratic model may therefore be seen as creating and taking advantage of stable and simple conditions. This makes it easier to achieve specialization and short run efficiency, and makes innovative change both undesirable and — as long as the stable conditions do not change — largely unnecessary. Consequently, there is little room for creativity or innovation in this context, except as a threat to the existing organization. As a result of the high degree of formalization in the bureaucratic model, organizational flexibility may be expected to be low. At the same time, if stable and simple operational conditions prevail, the need for such flexibility will also be low. Organizational diversity may also be expected to be low in such organizations, as a result of the highly specialized and segmented task structure. This means low values for both these important conditions for company creativity, organizational flexibility and diversity. Both the motivation for

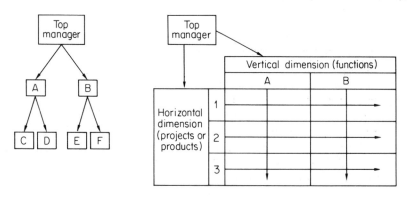

A. Bureaucratic Organization   B. Matrix Organization

Figure 3.1. Authority Relationships in Bureaucratic and Matrix Organizations

innovation and the ability to innovate may therefore be expected to be low, if bureaucratic elements predominate in the organization of a company.

In bureaucratic organizations there is therefore little need for company development strategies. Instead, the organization structure itself mainly determines what activities are carried out, both in the short and in the long run. Organization members, in their work capacity, more resemble passive machines, than active and creative human beings. The organization structure is basically a set of rules, rather than a collection of individuals and the inflexibility of these rules works against personal initiative and new ideas.

Other dysfunctional aspects of bureaucratic organizations have been stated by many writers, both before and after Weber (Merton, 1940; Selznick, 1949; Gouldner, 1954; Thompson, 1961; Crozier, 1964). The tendency to stress means, instead of goals, for instance, or the risk that control standards will encourage minimal participation. The vicious circle of control leading to more control, has also been pointed out, which of course is particularly serious when innovation is needed. For our purpose, however, the most interesting criticism is that which states that bureaucratic tendencies inhibit creativity (Thompson, 1969). We will be more concerned with this issue in Chapter 4.

Although Weber's organizational analysis is mostly concerned with bureaucratic structures, his analysis of other types of organizations is also of interest to our study. His view of organizations is an evolutionary one, with less formalized charismatic organizations changing over time to more formalized traditional and, finally, to bureaucratic organizations. This is in line with our emphasis on change over time in organization structure, as an integral part of the process of company innovation. But while Weber views this as part of a general historical trend towards more rational and efficient organization forms, the present study looks at organizational change as a company-specific reaction to environmental demand.

Today Weber's main thesis no longer seems to be generally valid. Instead the trend is towards less formalized organization forms, as a reaction to more complex and changing environments. Even though the need now is for a more differentiated view, Weber's general discussion is, however, still of value in understanding organizational change. Some comment on his evolutionary view (Weber, 1947) therefore is in place.

In charismatic organizations, according to Weber, the authority of the leader is based on his own personality. The influence is almost magical or religious, and from an economic point of view irrational. This type of organization is unstable due to its dependence on the leader, and when he dies the organization may be expected to become characterized, instead, by traditional authority. This 'routinization of charisma' implies the establishment of a social hierarchy, with hereditary leadership. It also means that to some extent impersonal leadership is established to give the organization stability over time. Under favourable conditions, as Weber sees them, this type of organization may develop into a bureaucracy, based on legal authority and without personal leadership.

Weber, thus, views charismatic personal leadership as primitive and irrational. In complex, changing environments, however, such leadership may be both necessary and desirable. Strong personal leadership may then be required to change highly formalized and no longer functional organizations into less formalized and more flexible ones. The change over time from relatively stable to highly changing environments, which Weber did not envisage, means that we are back at the starting point in his evolutionary scheme.

Charismatic organizations of a new type, which stimulate creativity and innovation, may therefore in complex and changing environments be a needed development of bureaucratic organizations. In environments of this type innovative change is necessary. Such change may be facilitated by a creative leader who understands the requirements of an uncertain environment, and changes the organization to reflect these needs.

3.3 Matrix model

The other basic model of organization structure which will be presented in contrast to the bureaucratic organization is the *Matrix Organization* (Kingdon, 1973; Galbraith, 1973; Knight, 1976). The characteristics of this model may be summarized in a number of points, chosen to correspond to the description of the bureaucratic model.

1. Instead of being based on a single, hierarchic system of relationships — as the bureaucratic model — the matrix model assumes a dual organization (Figure 3.1B). Two overlapping structures, both explicitly acknowledged by management, coexist.

2. One of these structures, the vertical one, corresponds to the traditional, hierarchic structure of the bureaucratic model. It is based on specialized competence and division of work (organizational differentiation). The other, the horizontal one, is based on the need for coordination of dependent activities (organizational integration).

3. The simultaneous existence of two formally recognized structures, a vertical one based on specialized functions and a horizontal one based on projects or products, means that a number of organization members have two superiors on the same level of organization. This may easily cause confusion in the case of conflicting orders, since the subordinate then does not know whom to follow, but also should lead to greater organizational flexibility.

4. Conflicts between members on the same level in an organization are preferably solved by interpersonal contacts and negotiation, rather than by being referred to a higher level in the vertical structure. This implies a lower degree of formalization than hierarchical bureaucratic structures.

5. Flexible and less detailed mechanisms of control (e.g. budgets) are preferred to closely specified orders from above.

Matrix organizations, therefore, may be seen as attempts to develop open and flexible organization structures, which make it easier to achieve a balance between the conflicting needs for specialization and coordinated development in complex and changing environments. Specialization, as we have noted before, is directed towards short run efficiency, while the need for coordinated development increases with the degree of innovative change. The need for a balance between specialization and coordination consequently also is a need for a balance between short run efficiency and long run development.

Organizational flexibility should tend to be higher in matrix organizations compared to bureaucratic ones, since organizational control is based on flexible, informal contacts between organization members, rather than inflexible, formal rules. By expanding and mixing knowledge and experience — via the spontaneous interaction of people and activities — matrix organizations should also tend to lead to high organizational diversity. Even on low levels in organizations, matrix organizations encourage the development of project groups and other interdepartmental groups and committees. This may be expected to broaden the experience and outlook of organization members, which, as we shall see in Chapter 4, is a major condition for company creativity. In addition, in matrix organizations, organizational diversity may well be enhanced by the company attracting and retaining creative individuals, who should find their management style more conductive to working in matrix organizations, than in bureaucratic ones. As we shall see in Chapter 4 such people usually have a broad and complex world view, and should therefore contribute to organizational diversity.

The matrix organization thus, in a general sense, recognizes the need to achieve a balance between development needs and efficiency, while the bureaucratic model emphasizes efficient operation under unchanging conditions. In the next section we will discuss a number of more specific models of organization structure, which in various degrees resemble the two basic models.

3.4 Applications of the basic models

So far in this chapter the discussion has intentionally been simplified and limited to two basic models of organization structure, the bureaucratic and the matrix organization. The approach has been to begin with these ideal constructions, to highlight their dominant features and give a better understanding of the basic mechanisms involved. In the real world, of course, we will find any number of more complicated and mixed organization structures (Walker and Lorsch, 1970; Galbraith, 1973; Horvath, 1976). The contention is, however, that they may be meaningfully and usefully described as more or less characterized by the defining characteristics of the basic models.

The basic overall variable employed to show differences in organization structure, is as we have noted before the degree of formalization. The basic models represent a high and intermediate level of formalization, represented by the bureaucratic and matrix model respectively. The interval from an intermediate to a very low level of formalization is more of theoretical than practical interest. The reason is that the concept of organization structure, by definition, implies formalization, and the absence of formalization, means that no structure exists.

It is possible to conceive of structures — for instance extreme cases of project organizations — which are less formalized than matrix organizations. In practice, however, project organizations tend to be special cases of matrix organizations. In our discussion of specific applications, the project organization will therefore be viewed as a type of matrix organization, rather than as an example of an even more unformalized and flexible organization form.

Functional organizations

Our first example of a specific organization structure is the traditional functional organization. As in the rest of this chapter, we will be mainly concerned with the overall organization. Within this overall structure a company may, and should, organize its activities differently within different departments, to reflect intracompany differences in task environment. It is important that we recognize the need for such differences, but when considering the company as a whole, the emphasis is on the overall structure. On a lower level of analysis, we may then apply the same type of reasoning to the design of smaller organizational units, such as departments or project groups. The basic functional design is shown in Figure 3.2A, while two variations of this structure, of special interest for our discussion, are shown in Figures 3.2B and 3.2C.

In the basic design, four functional departments are under direct supervision of the managing director. These departments are Production, Sales, Finance, and Research and Development. The department heads also have line responsibilities for their own departments, but for the sake of simplicity these relationships are omitted from the diagrams. As in the basic bureaucratic model each subordinate has one superior, from whom he receives orders and to whom he reports. This implies that there is clear specialization of function and each

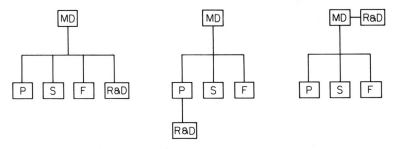

A. Functional Organization with Parallel R and D Department

B. Functional Department with R and D under Production

C. Line–Staff Organization with R and D as Staff Function

Figure 3.2. Examples of Functional and Line–Staff Organizations showing Different Location of Research and Development

executive is assumed to be competent within his area of responsibility. There is no distinction between specialized experts and general administrators in this model, which assumes that organizational position and the knowledge and competence to carry out the associated responsibilities coincide.

If we compare this situation with our previous discussion of the two basic organization structures, it is clear that bureaucratic tendencies predominate in functional organizations. The single hierarchy of vertical relationships and the clear specialization are defining characteristics of the basic bureaucratic model. The high degree of formalization necessary for these purposes should tend to lead to low organizational flexibility for functional organization structures. At the same time, as we have noted above, organizational diversity should tend to be low. The functional organization therefore may be expected to be unsuitable as an overall guide to organization structure in companies working in highly complex and changing environments.

Such environments are, for instance, usually characterized by a high rate of new product development. Within a functional organization structure such development may lead to very difficult coordination problems between, for instance, Production, Marketing, and Research and Development. Since direct communication and coordination between functions are not allowed — or at least made difficult — in this type of organization structure, the managing director has the obligation to resolve all conflicts between functional managers.

Functional organization structures thus lack direct coordination between operational departments, such as Production, and developmental departments, such as Research and Development. They may therefore be expected to tend to maintain existing market orientations and product lines. The operational departments essentially may be expected to lack the motivation and the developmental departments the production and marketing skills to conceive and carry out successful innovations. Only if the Managing Director is sufficiently wide ranging in skills and knowledge to bridge these gaps may companies with functional organization structure be expected to have successful strategies for innovative development. And if this is the case, the reliance on one person for innovative change will be a severe restriction, especially in large, complex companies working in highly changing environments.

By locating Research and Development under an operational department, usually Production, a closer connection between operational and development needs may be achieved (Figure 3.2B). But this connection will then probably tend to favour ongoing operations, rather than radical change. Organizational flexibility and diversity may hardly be expected to increase, compared to having Research and Development as a department directly under the Managing Director. It is more likely that organizational flexibility and diversity will decrease, as a result of the limited freedom and greater operational restrictions on Research and Development.

Attempts to increase organizational flexibility and diversity in functional organizations usually involve adding a horizontal staff dimension, to the vertical line of the hierarchic relationship (Figure 3.2C). This line–staff structure (Rhenman, Strömberg and Westerberg, 1963) implies distinguishing between an administrative, management role, and an advisory, specialist role. As we have noted before, the basic bureaucratic model makes no such distinction, instead it assumes that the two roles may be carried out successfully by one person, at any level of the organization. In matrix organizations, however, such a distinction is usually the basis for constructing a dual organization structure.

In line–staff organizations, however, the role of staff experts is limited by the fact that staff positions are not part of the formal hierarchy of executive responsibility. Instead, staff members are viewed as consultants to line executives. They provide information for decision making, but do not make actual decisions.

Such staff positions may, for instance, be concerned with research and development. By recruiting experts to these positions, organizational diversity may be increased, since they should broaden the knowledge basis of the company and contribute to new ideas. The organizational flexibility of the company — mainly affecting the likelihood of new ideas being implemented — will probably not be affected, however, since the functionally specialized hierarchy of decision making is retained. Coordination between functions will still probably be as difficult to achieve as before, as well as the implementation of company strategies for innovation. From the point of view of company creativity, a line or staff organization may therefore be viewed as an organization structure tending to widen the competence of a company, without tackling the problem of coordinating knowledge and making the organization more open to change.

In reality, however, line–staff organizations seldom function as intended. Instead, staff members usually get involved in actual decision making, and if this practice is formally recognized a dual organization structure is in effect introduced. This, then, means that the functional, line–staff organization changes into a matrix organization.

One way to increase organizational flexibility in a functional organization — without turning it into a matrix organization — is to build various organizational mechanisms for coordination into the structure. Examples of such mechanisms are temporary or permanent committees, for instance new product committees. By including people from different departments in such committees communication and coordination between different functional areas should be improved. By creating special positions or departments in the organization for coordination purposes, a more formal status may be given to these coordination efforts.

If people are specially recruited to perform coordinating activities as their main function, organizational flexibility will probably increase more, than if people are assigned to committees as part of their normal duties. There is some empirical evidence (Lawrence and Lorsch, 1967) that coordination is best carried out by individuals whose orientation and attitudes lie in between the values expressed by people holding the competing points of view. This, then, makes it easier for the coordinators to find solutions which are acceptable to all parties concerned.

Project organizations

By choosing a project organization a company achieves a very open and flexible structure. Project groups are then created for specific purposes and desolved when there no longer is a need for them. This type of structure, however, is usually not feasible as an overall design for organizing a company, even in highly changing and uncertain environments.

The obvious reason is the lack of permanent status which a strict project organization implies for the members of the organization. In such an organization members in principle are temporarily employed for specific projects. This is in variance with their needs for occupational security and professional careers. By combining a project structure with a functional structure, however, organization members may be given a more permanent status as experts, independent of their temporary assignments to project groups.

This in fact means implementing a matrix organization, and thereby balancing the need for flexibility in project work with the need for more long run stability in company personal planning. Particularly in research and development departments this type of matrix organization, combining a project and a functional structure, has clear advantages.

Venture organizations

Another alternative for companies who want to combine continuity in research efforts with diversity and flexibility in carrying out research, is to establish a semi-independent venture organization (Hill and Hlavacek, 1972; Rothwell, 1975) within the company. By making this a profit-centre, it can carry out commissioned R and D for operational divisions, which then may concentrate on manufacturing and marketing existing products. Such a venture organization may also develop new products which are not suitable for the company's own line of business. Resulting product rights and technical knowledge may then be sold or licensed to other companies. In this way a company may take advantage of ideas for new products, even when it cannot, or does not want to, make and market the actual products.

Venture organizations should help to create favourable conditions for company creativity. By radically separating on-going business from research and development, undue interference between the two can be minimized. The venture organization itself may be given an open structure to stimulate new ideas, by emphasizing organizational flexibility and diversity. Operational production and marketing problems, requiring a greater emphasis on closure and short run efficiency are in this type of structure transferred to the operational divisions, which may be more tightly designed to reflect this orientation.

A problem with this organizational set-up is to achieve coordination between the non-commissioned research carried out by the venture organization and the long term needs of the operational divisions. One way to achieve such coordination is to exchange personnel between the venture and operational divisions for shorter or longer periods of time. This should tend to increase organizational diversity for the company as a whole. It should also lead to a better understanding within the company, of the different problems confronting R and D and day-to-day operations.

Coordination between a venture division and operational divisions may, of course, also be attempted by similar means, for instance coordinating committees, as between different functional departments in a functional organization. At the same time, the need for such coordination should be smaller between divisions than between departments. The reason is that divisions are designed to be as self-contained and independent as possible, while functional departments have strong interdependencies which are maximized, rather than minimized, by the chosen design.

3.5 Two organizational classification models

In this section I will discuss two attempts in the organization literature to classify organizations in two basic categories. Similar to our company classification model presented in Chapter 2, these categories are intended to reflect differences in the ability of companies to respond to environmental change. The models are more partial, however, than our classification model, since they consider only differences in organization structure and not strategic differences. In other words, they assume that strategy follows structure. There is, therefore, no need as in our case to distinguish between a structural component — innovative potential — and a strategic component — innovative orientation — in analysing company development. In spite of this, these models are helpful to us in developing an understanding of the structural component of our more general model.

Mechanistic and organic organizations

Burns and Stalker (1961) have presented a classification of companies based on empirical studies of electronic and textile companies in England and Scotland. Following earlier ideas in the sociological literature they distinguish between two extreme types of organizations, mechanistic and organic.

Mechanistic organizations are assumed to be most appropriate to stable conditions and are characterized by the following:

1. The specialized differentiation of functional tasks into which the problems and tasks of the company as a whole are broken down.

2. Emphasis on the abstract nature of each individual task and the technical means to achieve these ends.

3. Coordination of functions on a given level of the organization are carried out by the immediate superiors.

4. Precise definitions and technical specifications are attached to each functional role.

5. Responsibility and functional position coincide (clear delegation of responsibility).

6. Hierarchic structure of control, authority and communication.

7. Knowledge of relevant company matters is concentrated at the top of the hierarchy, where final decisions are made (centralization of knowledge and decision making).

8. Tendency for vertical interaction between members of the company, i.e. between superior and subordinate.

9. Operations and working behaviour are governed by the instructions and decisions of superiors (centralization of work management).

10. Insistance on loyalty to the company and obedience to superiors.

11. Greater importance and prestige is attached to internal, local than to general, cosmopolitan knowledge, experience and skill.

Organic organizations, assumed to be appropriate to changing conditions, are characterized by the following:

1. The contributive nature of special knowledge and experience is emphasized.

2. The individual task is seen as set by the total situation of the company.

3. Individual tasks are continually adjusted and redefined through interaction with others.

4. No limited fields of responsibility, i.e. problems may not be avoided as being somebody else's responsibility.

5. Spread of commitment to the company beyond any technical definition.

6. A network structure of control, authority and communication

7. Omniscience no longer imputed to the head of the company. Knowledge of relevant factors may be located anywhere in the organization.

8. Lateral rather than vertical direction of communication within the organization. Consultation between people of different rank, rather than command.

9. Communication more consisting of information and advice, than instruction and decisions.

10. Commitment to the company's task and to technological progress is more highly valued than loyalty and obedience.

11. Affiliations and expertise valid in the external, technical and commercial environment of a company are accorded importance and prestige (cosmopolitism highly valued).

Burns and Stalker's classification is mainly based on the types of relationships (Burns and Stalker, 1961) between individual organization members, and the restrictions on these relationships stipulated by the organization structure. In our terminology their classification mainly refers to the limitations in innovative potential to which different organization structures lead. More closed, highly formalized, mechanistic structures lead to greater restrictions and less flexibility in the interplay between individual members, and thus to less innovative potential for the company as a whole, compared to less formalized and more open organic structures. Innovative orientation, on the other hand, is not explicitly considered in their classification scheme.

For this reason, as we have noted before, Burns and Stalker's classification model is more partial than ours. Their mechanistic organization is described in terms closely resembling Weber's bureaucratic model. The bureaucratic model, as we have seen, assumes that the organization structure, and not the organization members, determines the direction of organizational efforts. This, then, explains why there is no need for considering strategic choice in bureaucratic models.

In Burns and Stalker's classification scheme, innovative orientation and change are not explicitly ruled out in their definition of mechanistic organizations. If centrally decided by top management, innovative activities may be attempted. The lack of innovative potential, however, makes the successful implementation of such measures highly unlikely. In appropriate stable environments, on the other hand, the need for innovative change should tend to be low, and also the motivation for top management to consider such changes.

With regard to organic organizations, in appropriate complex and changing environments, innovative orientation and change are both necessary and possible. Burns and Stalker's classification scheme does not consider, however, organic organizations which lack the innovative orientation necessary for conceiving and carrying out such changes. Instead, they implicitly assume — as in the case of mechanistic organizations — that strategy and structure are in balance with each other, and with the needs of the environment.

Burns and Stalker thus essentially present a static, equilibrium view of company development. Or, in other words, they limit their attention to organizations in which both strategy and structure are appropriate to the environmental conditions in which they are active. But, as we have seen, even under given environmental conditions innovative companies may need to change their organization over time, to achieve successful development. And both positional and innovative companies may be confronted by changes in their internal or external environments which lead to a, perhaps temporary, lack of balance between strategy and structure, and between the company and its environment.

To analyse company development over time we therefore need a company classification model which considers both strategy and structure, and the interplay between the two. Latent positional/innovative companies, for instance, which in a static framework appear inappropriate both under stable and changing conditions, may be necessary transitory forms, when changing from one type to another. To make possible this type of dynamic analysis of company development, we need a more differentiated classification model than Burns and Stalker's dichotomy.

At the same time the classification of organizations as mechanistic or organic is of value to us in discussing organization structure. Similar to the bureaucratic model the mechanistic model gives content to what type of structure positional companies should tend to develop under stable conditions. The organic model — which is a highly open and flexible organization structure — may be viewed in relation to the matrix organization, which it resembles in many repects. It therefore is of interest when discussing suitable organization structure for innovative companies.

Static and dynamic organizations

Hage and Aiken (1970) have presented a classification model distinguishing between static and dynamic organizations, which in many respects is similar to Burns and Stalker's classification of mechanistic and organic organizations.

Static organizations are defined as organizations, the structure of which is characterized by low complexity, high centralization and high stratification.

Dynamic organizations, on the other hand, are characterized by high complexity, low centralization, low formalization and low stratification. They are thus the opposite of static organizations, with regard to these variables.

The variables describing static and dynamic organizations are reflected in both formal and informal structure. Complexity is measured by the number of occupations found in a company, and the extensiveness of training and intricacy of tasks performed. The formal component of complexity is training, for instance in schools, while the informal component is experience gained while actually carrying out the work involved. A larger number of occupations and a greater need for training and experience is assumed to lead to higher complexity in a company's organization structure.

It is interesting to compare Hage and Aiken's concept of complexity, with our concept of organizational diversity. In some instances greater complexity may lead to greater organizational diversity by increasing the variety of experience and skills in a company. But if training and experience lead to higher specialization for individual members, greater complexity may well instead lead to less organizational diversity. Complexity — as defined and measured by Hage and Aiken — if carefully used, may thus be one possible indicator, among others, of organizational diversity. By and large, however, this concept does not adequately reflect important differences between innovative and positional companies, and therefore will not be used in our study.

With regard to centralization, this is taken by Hage and Aiken to refer to the distribution of power. The higher the locus of power in the hierarchy tends to be, the more centralized it is. The formal aspect of centralization is authority and the informal aspect influence.

The concept of centralization is in practice highly elusive and difficult to measure in empirically meaningful ways. It is therefore not used by us to distinguish between positional and innovative companies. Instead it may be viewed as a factor which often, but not always, is reflected in the degree of formalization. In other words, highly formalized and closed companies may be expected to tend towards centralized decision making, as a result of their explicit recognition of formal authority. This, however, may be counteracted by informal channels of influence, which makes actual inferences of the distribution of company power difficult to draw. In our study the degree of formalization is used as the basic feature of organization structure, distinguishing between more open and more closed structures. Other aspects, such as centralization, are viewed as secondary factors of less interest to us.

Hage and Aiken also use the degree of formalization as an important variable in their classification model. They define it as the importance of rules in governing organizational behaviour. The formal component in this case is the written regulations and the informal component the accepted, but unwritten rules or customs. As a measure they suggest the number of rules or regulations, with a higher number denoting a higher degree of formalization.

This definition is consistent with our definition of formalization, as the extent to which the relationships and requirements of the formal structure are explicitly and clearly spelt out in detail. But again it is more limited in its operationalization, by referring only to the number of regulations, and not to how detailed they are in restricting acceptable behaviour.

The mixing together by Hage and Aiken of formal and informal aspects — as in the case of the other definitions — also makes it difficult to use their approach to discuss the degree of formalization in different organization structures. We, instead, have chosen to distinguish initially between formal and informal relationships, but have assumed that if the formal structure is appropriately designed, informal relationships will tend to support the formal ones. This, then, means that we do not need a separate discussion of informal relationships in our analysis.

The final variable in Hage and Aiken's classification scheme is the degree of stratification. This stresses the importance of rewards, and refers to the way in which rewards are distributed among jobs and occupations. The greater the differences between levels, and the difficulties in moving from one level to the next, the greater the degree of stratification. The formal component of this variable is status differences, while the informal component is differences in prestige. The former is more directly manifested in salary and other tangible benefits while the latter is more indirectly indicated by the rug on the office floor or other symbols of company standing.

The degree of stratification, while not directly considered in our analysis, is interesting against the background of our discussion of different organization structures in this chapter. Matrix organizations, for instance, make possible a more equal and democratic reward system, than bureaucratic organizations. Their multiple structure makes it possible to give a larger number of employees a high formal status in the organization. Creative research workers without administrative qualifications or interests may, for instance, achieve formal recognition in parallel positions to functional managers. Rewarding and motivating creativity in other lines of company work than traditional management, for instance in research and development, should therefore be facilitated by a relatively low level of stratification.

This, then, should be a desirable feature of innovative companies. In positional companies, on the other hand, a high degree of stratification may be necessary to motivate top managers to accept the individual responsibility and work level, which higher positions may well demand in these types or organizations. Stimulating overall company creativity by a low level of stratification will in these companies probably be viewed as unnecessary and perhaps even seen as threatening the desired stability in company operations.

Comparison between the classification models

There are great similarities between Burns and Stalker's classification of companies as mechanistic or organic and Hage and Aiken's as static or dynamic. The basis for these classification schemes differ however. The similarities may therefore be viewed more as an indication of the need for this type of general classification, than as due to similar arguments in devising the schemes. As we have mentioned before, Burns and Stalker base their distinction on empirical studies of the relationships between organization members, while Hage and Aiken's distinction is based on axiomatic relationships between organizational means and ends. In this sense our approach more closely resembles Hage and Aiken's analysis, than Burns and Stalker's.

Both our discussion of positional companies and Hage and Aiken's discussion of static organizations, assume that short run efficiency — based on high production volume and little product change — is the dominating company goal. With regard to innovative companies and dynamic organizations, company and product development become of utmost importance, in addition to the need for short run efficiency. Both our own and Hage and Aiken's discussions stress the varying emphasis on efficiency and development in the two basic situations, and the need for a balance between these goals which reflects environmental needs.

As in the case of mechanistic and organic organizations, the classification of companies as static and dynamic is more partial, however, than our concepts of positional and innovative companies. As we have noted before, these alternative classifications only consider structural variation and not strategic variation. Hage and Aiken (1970) explicitly acknowledge this in stating that they emphasize structural properties, and do not consider company leadership. At the same time they admit that differences in leadership may account for the differences which they ascribe to structural variation. Our approach is an attempt to resolve this difficulty, by considering both structural properties and company leadership in our classification. This is done by our choice of basic concepts, innovative potential and innovative orientation.

Due to their reliance on structural properties, both Burns and Stalker's discussion of mechanistic and organic organizations, and Hage and Aiken's discussion of static and dynamic organizations, are of main interest to us in focusing on differences in organization structure, which may distinguish between positional and innovative companies. Ideally, positional companies should have organization structures similar to those attributed to mechanistic and static organizations, and innovative companies structures similar to what is said to characterize organic and dynamic organizations. From our point of view, however, these structural differences are not sufficient to account for company development, at least not with regard to innovative companies in complex and changing environments, which require company creativity. We, then, not only need to consider structural constraints on creativity, but also its active component, innovative orientation and strategies to achieve such an orientation.

3.6 Summary of Chapter 3

In this chapter I discuss the design of the company's organization structure, always bearing in mind the need to achieve a suitable balance in a variety of environments between the demands of short run efficiency and long run innovative development. The achievement of short run efficiency is facilitated by stable and simple conditions, while the need for innovative development increases with growing complexity and change in the company's environment.

A high degree of formalization in the organization structure seems likely to provide favourable conditions for short run efficiency, because of the clearcut and detailed advance control of operations and of the work of the various individuals involved. At the same time this kind of close control will probably lead to less flexibility in the organization, since the design of the organization structure makes it more difficult for the company to change the direction of its operations quickly and radically. While it facilitates the achievement of short run efficiency, a high degree of formalization in the organization structure is likely to make it difficult to implement the kind of discontinuous changes that are part of the innovative development necessary in complex and changing environments.

But organizational flexibility, due to a low degree of formalization, may not only facilitate the implementation of innovative change. It may also, as we shall see in our discussion of company creativity, help to provide favourable conditions for conceiving of and formulating successful strategies for change. By making possible more spontaneous interaction between organization members and activities, organizational flexibility may lead to organizational diversity — broad and variegated knowledge and experience — which is a basic requirement of individual and company creativity.

Two basic models of organization structure are discussed in this chapter. The first, the bureacratic organization, provides a prototype of the closed kind of structure characterized by a high degree of formalization and a low degree of organizational flexibility and diversity. This model is geared chiefly towards the achievement of short run efficiency and is therefore most satisfactory as a basis for designing an organization structure suitable to continuous operations in a stable and simple environment. The bureaucratic organization model is therefore compatible with the principles of the traditional economic theory of the firm, although the company's internal organization is not explicitly dealt with in this theory.

The second basic model, the matrix organization, provides an example of an open organization structure with a relatively low degree of formalization and a relatively high degree of organizational flexibility and diversity. In comparison with the bureaucratic model this model makes better allowance for a company's need for long term innovative development in a complex and changing environment. At the same time it is possible to take into account the need for short run efficiency in day-to-day operations. These two aspects are considered in a dual organization stucture, where the conflicting requirements of various activities can be taken into account, although priorities have not been regulated in the formal structure. Instead it is assumed that conflicting claims will be continually weighed against one another in personal interaction between organization members. Compared with a bureaucratic system of impersonal control exerted through the organization structure, this sort of system makes it easier to adapt activities quickly to changing conditions.

In this chapter I also describe some specific types of structures — functional, line–staff project and venture organizations — illustrating that in practice we will find a continuum of organization structures, all of which represent variations of our basic models.

The functional organization most closely resembles the basic bureaucratic model, while the others represent various attempts to increase organizational flexibility and diversity. Along this scale the pure project organization can be regarded as the most extreme form, is which flexibility has been carried so far that continuity tends to disappear. Ultimately the organization becomes a temporary collection of people working together in groups within the framework of individual projects. When projects are completed the groups dissolve, and the organization ceases to exist. If there is to be any continuity of action and security for the organization members, a project structure therefore has to be combined with some other type of structure — for example a functional structure. If these structures are on equal terms as regards authority and decision making, we then have a matrix organization.

At the end of this chapter I look briefly at two company classification models that appear in the organization literature. Like our company classification model in Chapter 2 they are intended to reflect differences between companies appropriate to stable or changing environments.

However, the suggested categories — Burns and Stalker's mechanistic–organic, and Hage and Aiken's static–dynamic organizations — are not as differentiated as the company forms suggested in Chapter 2. Basically they are only concerned with differences in organization structures and they take no account of strategy differences. This prevents any dynamic analysis of the interplay between strategy and structure — which is emphasized in the present work.

Nevertheless, the categories suggested by these authors are of value to our analysis, since they enrich our understanding of the implications of organization structure for company development. Burns and Stalker's classification is interesting above all in its description of important factors in the organization structure, which are likely to affect the company's innovative potential, while the chief interest of Hage and Aiken's classification lies in the suggestion of possible empirical indicators for several of the factors.

As in the case of mechanistic and organic organizations, the classification of companies as static and dynamic is more partial, however, than our concepts of positional and innovative companies. As we have noted before, these alternative classifications only consider structural variation and not strategic variation. Hage and Aiken (1970) explicitly acknowledge this in stating that they emphasize structural properties, and do not consider company leadership. At the same time they admit that differences in leadership may account for the differences which they ascribe to structural variation. Our approach is an attempt to resolve this difficulty, by considering both structural properties and company leadership in our classification. This is done by our choice of basic concepts, innovative potential and innovative orientation.

Due to their reliance on structural properties, both Burns and Stalker's discussion of mechanistic and organic organizations, and Hage and Aiken's discussion of static and dynamic organizations, are of main interest to us in focusing on differences in organization structure, which may distinguish between positional and innovative companies. Ideally, positional companies should have organization structures similar to those attributed to mechanistic and static organizations, and innovative companies structures similar to what is said to characterize organic and dynamic organizations. From our point of view, however, these structural differences are not sufficient to account for company development, at least not with regard to innovative companies in complex and changing environments, which require company creativity. We, then, not only need to consider structural constraints on creativity, but also its active component, innovative orientation and strategies to achieve such an orientation.

CHAPTER 4

From Individual to Company Creativity

4.1 Introduction

There are almost as many ways of defining creativity as there are writers on the subject. For our purpose creativity may be viewed as new insight which points to better ways of dealing with reality. This ties in with our definition of innovation in Chapter 1, which as we remember was taken to mean radical, discontinuous change. Successful innovations therefore depend on creativity, and we need to provide favourable conditions for creativity, when radical changes are necessary or desirable.

In other words, creativity is seen as the cause and successful innovation as the effect. In order to understand and influence innovation we therefore need to start with the creative process and its requirements. Research on creativity (Anderson, 1959; Taylor and Barron, 1963; Vernon, 1970) supports the basic idea put forward here, that it is possible in advance to identify and control a number of factors which are essential to creative performance. We do not merely need to wait and see what the results will be when venturing into new areas. The probability of success may instead be actively increased by our establishing and maintaining a creative problem solving environment.

In this book we are mainly interested in company creativity and innovation (Steiner, 1965; Sandkull, 1970). A necessary basis for understanding company creativity is, however, individual creativity. To begin with we will therefore focus on what we know about individual creativity, and subsequently try to extend the discussion to the company level. This approach is both necessary and desirable. It is necessary because we know very little about company creativity as such, and it is desirable because the crucial determinant of company creativity is individual though and action. When passing from the individual to the company level we need, of course, also to consider group factors and the organization of people and resources, which was our focus of interest in Chapter 3. If the basic conditions for individual creativity are lacking, however, no organization can compensate for this by merely reorganizing its resources.

On the other hand organizational and economic factors may well act as restraints on individual creativity, and prevent the results of individual creativity from being realized in company action. It is even likely that some organizational factors which are favourable at the early stages of the creative process — for instance diversity (Wilson, 1966) and decentralization — will make it more difficult to implement the results. This is a dilemma for companies faced with the need to innovate, and a major concern in this chapter is to indicate ways of resolving this problem.

Among psychologists, individual creativity used to be a highly neglected area of research, due to prevailing research doctrines — behaviourism and stimulus–reponse theories — emphasizing measurement and predictability (May, 1959). This, by and large, precluded creativity from consideration, since it is an elusive and complicated phenomena, difficult to precisely define and control.

During the last decades the situation has, however, radically changed and research on creativity has become accepted and grown in importance. This has been accompanied by a change in emphasis in explaining this type of intellectual activity. Instead of viewing creativity as essentially a passive, random process of association, it is increasingly seen as the result of active, directed thought (Cropley 1967; Bolton, 1972). This type of cognitive approach to creativity makes it easier to understand both the creative process and individual differences in creativity, and underlies both the general discussion of creativity in this chapter and the cognitive model of decision making presented in Chapter 6.

In the study of individual creativity two research traditions have existed side by side without much interaction and no integrated framework combining the results from these two approaches has been developed. The first is concerned with analysing the creative process and the second with studying the characteristics of creative individuals and their environments. Since both are of interest to us they will be dealt with in the following, leading up to the discussion of company creativity, which is our main concern in this chapter.

4.2 The creative process

Generally speaking, we may regard the individual creative process (Figure 4.1) as a question of first widening and then narrowing the constraints inherent in formulating and solving a problem. This process may be divided into a number of stages:

1. Preparation
2. Incubation
3. Illumination (Insight)
4. Verification

Even if the number of stages varies most analysts of the creative process basically employ the same type of model (Poincaré, 1913; Wallas, 1926). The process begins with a period of preparation when material is collected from a wide variety of sources. This involves a conscious effort to open up the universe of discourse and broaden the problem perspective. At this stage the ideas are usually not verbal (Wertheimer, 1959; Koestler, 1964, but visual and rather vague. This vagueness, however, is constructive by delimiting the problem without prematurely locking the analysis in fixed directions. In this way flexibility is combined with guidance in the problem solving efforts. The

Stages	Requirements
Preparation	Openness to experience
	Tolerance for ambiguity
	Willingness to redefine concepts
	Divergent thought processes
	Intuitive ability
Incubation	(imagination)
	Sub-conscious data processing
	Independence
	Psychological freedom
	Psychological safety
Illumination	Ability to switch from intuitive
	to analytical patterns of thought
	Critical attitude
	Convergent thought processes
Verification	Analytical ability
	(intelligence)

Figure 4.1. Stages and Important Requirements of the
Individual Creative Process

concepts used are open ended (Bannister and Fransella, 1971), which makes it easy both to develop new concepts and change the meaning of old ones, as the definition and formulation of the problem evolves over time.

The emphasis in the preparation stage thus is on a wide, unformalized, intuitive type of thinking (compare Chapter 7). A total 'gestalt' perspective dominates over a more limited, detailed focus (Wertheimer, 1959). At this stage it is also important that resistance towards redefining existing concepts is not too strong (Bruner, 1965).

Exactly what concepts are chosen, or how precise they are, is of secondary interest. The main thing is that they provide tentative guidance without blocking new insight.

Divergent thinking, which explores many possibilities, rather than convergent thinking, which concentrates on a single line of reasoning, should therefore be of great value during the preparation stage. Most tests of creativity and techniques to promote creativity, for instance brain storming (Osborn, 1953), are primarily intended to measure or stimulate divergent thinking. We must keep in mind, however, that this type of thinking is not sufficient for creativity. Convergent thinking is also necessary, and at later stages of the creative process is of primary importance.

The often seemingly resultless preparation period is followed by an incubation period, when conscious concentration on the problem ends and instead subconscious data processing may be assumed to take place (Ehrenzweig, 1967). A large number of combinations of though elements are then gone through, perhaps in a dream-like process. In addition to subjective reports by creative individuals stressing the importance of an incubation period for creativity, experiments have been carried out which support this (Fulgosi and Guilford, 1968; Dreistadt, 1969).

If the subconscious thought processes are successful, the incubation period leads to insight, — usually sudden — discovery of previously unrelated ideas, conceived as a solution to the problem. Often this 'effective surprise' (Bruner, 1965) is accompanied by a strong intuitive feeling that the belief is justified. The subjective criteria for this belief, which surprisingly often turns out to be correct, is one of the most important, but also most evasive elements of the creative process. One type of criteria, often suggested by mathematicians, is simplicity and elegance. Simple solutions also in practice often turn out to be better than complex solutions, and this may then be seen as a pragmatic test of their usefulness.

This leads us to the final, verification stage, which is concerned with formal control of the results against objective criteria. It is mainly during this stage that traditional scientific reasoning, based on deductive logic and isolated cause–effect relationships, is applicable. In spite of this, the type of formal analysis useful during this stage is often viewed as characteristic of and desirable for all types and stages of problem solving.

4.3 Internal and external factors related to individual creativity

The other type of research on creativity deals with characteristics of the individual and his environment related to creativity. This type of research is valuable both for the purpose of helping individuals to be more creative and for judging creative capacity.

An attempt to formulate a number of general hypotheses relating characteristics both of the individual and his environment to creative performance has been made by Rogers (1959). These hypotheses are particularly interesting for our purpose, since they have interesting implications for company creativity.

Rogers assumes that the main motivation for individual creativity is self-actualization. He claims that everyone has this desire, although it may be more or less repressed. According to him it is mainly in individuals open to new experience that creativity — in the positive sense in which we use the term — may be expected to occur. Roger himself distinguishes between good and bad creativity, and believes that suppression of important phases of experience leads to distorted, that is destructive creativity.

Rogers then formulates a number of general hypotheses about the relationships between internal psychological characteristics of individuals and creativity. He believes that creativeness (measured by the number of significant novel and original products) will increase when:

1. Individuals show greater openness to experience
2. They have a more internal focus of evaluation

3. They have a greater ability to toy with elements and concepts

By openness to experience Rogers means lack of rigidity in concepts, beliefs, perceptions and hypotheses, tolerance for ambiguity and the ability to deal with conflicting information without forcing closure upon the situation.

An internal locus of evaluation means that the individual himself determines the value of a creative product and is not influenced by the praise or criticism of others. A greater ability to toy with elements and concepts (ideas, colours, shapes, relationships) is viewed as less important than the other two factors, but still a necessary condition.

We may compare the above hypotheses with what we have previously said about the creative process. The first requirement — openness to experience — should be particularly important during the preparation stage, by broadening the area of investigation. The second — internal locus of evaluation — and third — ability to toy with elements and concepts — should be crucial during the incubation and illumination stages. Freedom from conventional thought and a playful attitude should then provide favourable conditions for generating new insight, by increasing the spontaneous interaction between elements and the willingness to entertain new and unusual ideas.

With regard to external environmental conditions favourable to creativity, Rogers believes that the creativeness of an individual may be expected to increase when:

1. The individual experiences greater psychological safety.
2. The individual experiences greater psychological freedom.

Greater psychological safety may be achieved in three ways. First, by accepting the individual for what he is. Second, by providing a climate in which external evaluation is absent, to prevent the need for defensiveness which always leads to less awareness of experience. Third, by understanding empathically, that is accepting the individual from his own point of view, which together with the other two factors leads to a maximum of psychological safety.

Psychological freedom, the second of the two environmental factors influencing creativity, means freedom for the individual symbolically to express his personality in thinking and feeling. This does not mean freedom to realize everything in action, since society may and should restrict behaviour. But it means freedom for the individual to explore the possibilities open to him.

Rogers' hypotheses appear, in general, to be consistent with what we know from empirical studies. Creative individuals, for instance, apparently prefer complex and seemingly unbalanced visual representations, which require an open and non-committed mind to appreciate. Less creative individuals tend to prefer more symmetrical and stereotype pictures (Barron, 1955). This may be seen as supporting Rogers' emphasis on the importance of openness to experience for creativity. Research on cognitive styles also indicates that highly creative individuals tend to have more open and less creative individuals more restricted ways of perceiving and constructing reality (Bolton, 1972; Shouksmith, 1970).

Rogers' assumption that creative individuals have an internal locus of evaluation, that is are more independent and less likely to accept outside authority, finds support in many studies. Roe, for instance, concludes in her study of 64 scientists that independence probably is the strongest single factor accounting for creative success (Roe, 1952).

Playfulness has also been emphasized by other researchers as an important condition for creativity (March, 1976). In one instance, it has even been regarded — in combination with richness of ideas — as the most important determinant of creativeness (Wallach and Kogan, 1965).

Turning to Rogers' hypotheses about external environment factors affecting creativity, we may find some empirical support. With regard to psychological safety it has, for instance, been shown by experiments that the absence of external evaluation during the early stages of the creative process (deferred judgement) significantly increases idea production (Parnes and Meadow, 1959; Meadow, Parnes and Reese, 1959). With regard to psychological freedom there are results indicating that creative individuals are less disciplined in their thoughts and more inclined to freely express their views, and at the same time more likely to accept the same type of behaviour in others (Barron, 1955).

Later on in this chapter Rogers' hypotheses will be used in discussing company creativity. We must not forget, however, that these conclusions primarily apply to the early stages of the creative process. As we have noted before the later stages require quite different conditions for success. It is then a question of achieving closure, rather than openness, in the creative process. This leads to quite different psychological and organizational requirements and to a need for flexibility in designing favourable conditions for creativity.

4.4 Group interaction and creativity

Before dealing directly with company creativity it is of interest to consider the effects of group interaction on the creative process. This may be seen as a factor intervening between individual and company creativity.

The type of group we are mainly interested in in this connection is the small group. This is an informal group of spontaneously interacting individuals, with a common interest in constructively dealing with a set of problems. We are interested in such groups belonging to a larger organization, which may or may not formally recognize their existance.

Since group interaction is a factor in determining company creativity and innovation, we need to try to determine its relative importance. As we have seen in Chapter 2 companies may try to activate and control group processes — for instance by their choice of organization structure — and this is an important aspect of organizational strategy. Matrix organizations, for instance, are designed to stimulate and guide informal group processes towards achieving overall company objectives.

What, then, characterizes group interaction and distinguishes it from individual problem solving? Drawing on the literature we will make the following general assumptions (Crosby, 1968; Thompson, 1969; Krech, Crutchfield and Ballachey, 1962):

1. Groups, by joining together people with different skills and knowledge,

usually represent a broader range of competence and interests, than single individuals.

2. Comparisons and confrontations between different points of view take place more easily in a group setting, than in the mind of an individual.

3. Groups usually have less fixed and more complex criteria for acceptable solutions than individuals.

4. In group problem solving, ideas have to be more clearly formulated and expressed, to facilitate communication between members, than in individual problem solving.

If we examine the first point, its positive influence during the early part of the creative process should be obvious. Together with the confrontations and comparisons between views indicated in the second point, the broad and diverse coverage of ideas which a group may achieve, compared to individual problem solvers, should lead to favourable initial conditions for creativity.

To a certain extent individuals may compensate for a more limited focus by reading what others have written. The confrontation between different points of view will then, however, in most instances, probably be less sharp and also less directly related to the specific issue, compared to what may be achieved through group interaction.

The third point should also indicate an advantage for group interaction, during the early part of the creative process. The more ambiguous, multidimensional criteria employed by groups, compared to individuals, in evaluating solutions, should counteract premature fixation of the analysis. An awareness of alternative criteria should also make it easier for group members to accept initial vagueness, apparent contradictions and deferred judgement in the creative process, all of which as we have noted before, are desirable attributes of early problem solving.

Group interaction, however, may also have negative effect on creativity, if we consider the fourth point. This is because group communication is a more fixed and less open-ended way of handling ideas, than individual thought processes. Because of the need for understanding each other, group members cannot express their intuitive ideas as spontaneously and freely in a group setting, as when they themselves work through a problem.

In this respect individual thought processes are better suited for handling new ideas, than group interaction (March and Simon, 1958). As we remember from our treatment of the creative process, intuitive vagueness is constructive at an early stage of the creative process, while expressing ideas clearly for communication purposes requires that such vagueness be eliminated.

At the verification stage, however, analytical closure — involving clear formulation and communication of results — is essential to success. Group interaction, by making necessary and facilitating this, will then be an aid to creativity.

Summing up what we have said so far about group interaction and creativity, we may conclude that group interaction probably is most favourable to creativity at very early stages — when broadening the area of investigation is essential — and at late stages — when clear formulation and communication is needed for testing the results. At the intermediary and most crucial stage — when combining previously unrelated ideas to a new constructive solution — individual thought processes probably dominate in importance.

The more we need radical solutions, the more pronounced the need for independent individual thought should tend to be. Extreme and divergent views put forward by creative individuals may be modified, or eliminated, if they are evaluated in a group setting. If companies want to become more innovative, emphasizing individual rather than group problem solving, may therefore be a worthwhile effort. Small companies are often claimed to be more innovative than large companies, and, while this is difficult to prove, one reason could be that small companies, more than large companies, tend to emphazise individual problem solving and decision making.

Another way in which group interaction may influence creativity is by its effect on motivation. Group cohesiveness and group homogeneity are two factors which are of interest in discussing this question. Group cohesiveness refers to the holding effect of groups on their members. If cohesiveness is high, members are attracted to each other, and the group tends to withstand pressures to dissolve. Group homogeneity refers to similarities among group members, for instance in values, experience or formal education.

Certain dimensions of group homogeneity have been shown to effect group cohesiveness (Blau and Scott, 1963; Crosby, 1968). High cohesiveness in turn appears to be related to greater psychological safety, self actualization and willingness among group members to accept the collective goals of the group and influence from other group members. From the group's point of view cohesiveness apparently also tends to lead to more consistent reactions and more intensive communications between group members, as we have noted above.

This leads to a dilemma in constructing a creative group climate. On the one hand high group cohesiveness is desirable, since it may be expected directly to motivate group members to be more creative, by increasing their feeling of psychological safety and self-actualization. When cohesiveness is high the individual evidently identifies more directly with what the group does and achieves greater satisfaction from group action. At the same time he is not alone responsible for possible failures, which is reassuring.

On the other hand, one factor which is important for high cohesiveness — group homogeneity — in itself may be expected to lessen the likelihood for creativity, by restricting diversity. Group heterogeneity, rather than homogeneity, thus should directly be favourable to creativity, by making groups more inventive (Hoffman, 1969), while homogeneity on the other hand may indirectly have desirable motivational effects by making groups more cohensive.

An added problem is that group interaction and cohesiveness evidently is facilitated by clear goals and precise problem descriptions (Raven and Rietsema, 1957), which as we have noted before, tend to diminish the likelihood of novel solutions being discovered. Group cohesiveness, too, may thus create tendencies both towards a more creative group climate, by creating favourable motivational conditions, and towards a less creative climate, by restricting outlook.

Resolving this dilemma requires a differentiated, conditional view of the importance of group interaction for creativity. The composition of groups should vary over time and group characteristics should depend on what stage the creative process is in. Early in the process loosely joined groups of a temporary nature, and heterogenous from the point of view of the problem considered, should be most suitable. They should provide both flexibility in problem solving and diversity in outlook, which as we have seen is essential for success at the preparation stage. Later, during the verification stage, cohesive homogeneous groups should be better suited, by making it easier to focus on, critically test and successfully implement solutions. During the critical, intermediate illumination period, individual efforts are most likely, however, to lead to insight, as we have stated above.

Also, we need a pluralistic view of group leadership to promote creativity (Thompson, 1969). Democratic leadership with spontaneously changing leaders in response to situational need should provide needed flexibility in this respect during early stages of problem solving.

Actual, rather than formal qualifications, then should determine what authority to follow on any specific issue. During the verification state — and when promoting and implementing accepted solutions — more permanent and authoritarian leadership may be necessary, however, to provide continuity and concentration in efforts.

4.5 Different modes of company problem solving

When discussing company creativity we will focus on different modes of company problem solving and their implications for company decision making. These different ways of viewing and dealing with problems will be seen in relation to the requirements for achieving new knowledge, which we have

Causal	Data basis	
relationships	Explicit and systematic	Implicit and intuitive
Explicit and systematic	Formal planning	Theoretical analysis
Implicit and intuitive	Empirical data investigation	Intuitive assessment

Figure 4.2. Modes of Company Problem Solving

Mode of problem solving	Characteristics
Intuitive assessment	Implicit and intuitive data basis and conclusions Overall widening of problem area Informational diversity and richness Speed and flexibility in reaching conclusions
Empirical data investigation	Explicit and systematic data basis Implicit and intuitive conclusions Empirical narrowing of problem area Flexibility in arranging and rearranging data
Theoretical analysis	Explicit and systematic conclusions Intuitive and implicit data basis Theoretical narrowing of problem area Flexibility and generality in reaching conclusions
Formal planning	Explicit and systematic data basis and conclusions Maintaining overall perspective Clear and operational objectives Coordination of efforts

Figure 4.3. Characteristics of Different Modes of Company Problem Solving

discussed in connection with the individual creative process. There are differences, however, in emphasis and content between individual and company creativity, which must be recognized. Both are dependent on individual thought processes, but company, more than individual creativity demands that we distinguish between and integrate complex problems and activities involving many individuals. This makes company-specific factors — the organization of the company and its economic resources — highly important in determining company creativity. Individual creativity is more concerned with isolated thought processes, and while overall company factors may impede or stimulate these processes, they are not by definition crucial to success, as in the case of company creativity.

The basis for our discussion of company problem solving is differences in how companies collect and evaluate information, what we may call different modes of problem solving (Figures 4.2 and 4.3). *Intuitive assessment* is when both the data basis and the causal relationships are implicit and intuitive. *Empirical data investigation* is when the data basis is explicit and systematic, but the causal relationships implicit and intuitive. *Theoretical analysis* is when the data basis is implicit and intuitive, but the causal relationships explicit and systematic. *Formal planning* finally, is when both the data basis and the causal relationships are explicit and systematic. (Compare the cognitive model of decision making in Chapter 7.)

Intuitive assessment

In the case of intuitive assessment, companies are thus open and flexible both with regard to what data they use and how they employ the data in reaching conclusions. We may compare this with the initial, preparatory stage of the individual creative process, with the difference that the company rather than the individual is now the problem solving unit.

Sometimes intuitive assessment emphasizing the overall possibilities rather than precise implications of company action may lead to final decisions without further structuring of the problem or systematic data collection. Indeed, this may even at times be desirable, since there is some evidence that intuition under certain conditions is more appropriate than analysis in reaching conclusions. Empirical experiments (Peters and Hammond, 1974) indicate that intuition tends to lead to approximately correct solutions, which are seldom exactly right, but almost never radically wrong. Formal analysis, on the other hand, tends to lead to solutions which are either precisely right or way off the mark.

Applied to company decision making these results indicate that in situations where the loss involved in making a radically wrong decision is great, intuitive assessment may be preferable to analytical problem solving. The marginal benefits to the company of analytical accuracy, if the basic approach is right, may then not be worth the risk of total miscalculation, if the analysis leads off in the wrong direction. As we have noted before restricting the problem solving area at an early stage by imposing analytical rigour, will make it difficult to change the line of reasoning later. Intuitive assessment by maintaining flexibility and overview is more adaptive in this sense.

The above line of reasoning can help to explain why highly important and risky company decisions, for instance investments in new lines of business, may in practice be decided on a rather intuitive basis. This is in contrast to what is usually recommended by operations researchers and other analytically oriented management theorists. They generally stress the need to systematically collect and process information as the basis for rational decision making. Against the background of our approach this emphasis on accuracy and clear-cut conclusions is commendable, if the timing is right. At such moments in the problem solving process when flexibility rather than rigour is called for, analytical precision may, however, impede rather than facilitate creativity.

Intuitive assessment — either as an end in itself or as a starting point for more refined analysis — will be best suited for unstructured problems (Mintzberg, Raisinghani and Théorât 1976), the content and implications of which are not well understood. Grasping the problem then is the main concern, which requires an open and searching mind. An example of such a problem area, which will be dealt with in Chapter 6, is company strategies for R and D. To be successful in generating new products such strategies require a wide and open, intuitive approach in searching for and initially evaluating ideas.

In intuitive assessment neither the problem area itself, nor the data basis, thus are clearly defined. Decision makers therefore, need to be open to experience, independent and willing to try new avenues of thought to succeed in this type of problem solving. As we have noted in our discussion of the individual creative process this is necessary if they are to conceive of constructive solutions in the absence of clear guidelines and immediately apparent ways of attacking a problem.

Designing problem solving groups to widen, rather than narrow the area of investigation, also is important in this connection, which according to our previous discussion in this chapter implies loose and heterogeneous problem solving groups with democratic situation-determined leadership. In practice committees are often used to achieve such open and flexible groups. New Product or Business Development Committees may, for instance, be set up with representatives for various functional areas such as marketing and R and D and group membership and leadership may vary over time to achieve flexibility and diversity in problem treatment. In addition creative techniques, such as brain storming, are often used as aids in expanding individual and group awareness of the problem area. Outside experts and consultants may also be employed to widen the scope of the investigation, as we shall see in Chapter 8 with respect to company strategies for R and D.

With regard to information content intuitive problem solving should be facilitated by informational richness and diversity. Complexity and ambiguity (March and Olsen, 1976) may be an advantage in this connection by stimulating creative individuals and making possible many different interpretations of the same data. Such informational richness may for instance be achieved by wide and extensive coverage of the external environment (Mintzberg, 1973a) and decentralized search patterns. Broad following up of technological advances and close market contact to monitor changes in buyer preferences are examples of this type of search. In the marketing literature emphasizing broad needs rather than narrowly defined products is called the new marketing concept (Kotler, 1967, and this is in line with our emphasis on broadening the problem perspective as an aid to intuitive problem solving. This does not mean, however, that such an approach is desirable under all problem solving conditions, as many marketing experts appear to believe.

The intuitive mode of company problem solving and decision making should also be facilitated by a relatively unformalized organization structure and a wide range of attitudes and knowledge in the company (high organizational flexibility and diversity). This should tend to lead both to flexibility in collecting and evaluating information and to favourable conditions for the transformation of informational richness into creative company action.

In the terminology of Chapter 2 this means a high innovative potential and —

if the other conditions for success in intuitive assessment are satisfied — a good chance that the company will be able to develop a clear innovative orientation, and thus become an innovative company.

Empirical data investigation

If applying the intuitive mode leads not to a final decision, but instead to a felt need for systematically collecting empirical data, another mode of company problem solving and decision making is indicated. This mode, empirical data investigation, requires that the data basis is explicit and systematic, but the causal relationships connecting the data fragments and making the picture intelligible are still implicit and intuitive.

To fill in the missing pieces in the puzzle, data is systematically collected, but the overall framework is given. This is in contrast to the more explorative type of data collection, which is used in the intuitive mode to build up the overall picture rather than fill in the details. As example of this type of empirically constrained but theoretically open problem solving is market investigation, as usually conceived and carried out by companies themselves, or outside consultants.

Companies then know what type of data they want to collect, but have no detailed and systematic, theoretical approach to analyse the data. They, for instance, usually try to estimate their market shares, but seldom have any clear analytical models for relating this type of data to company performance. Instead this is done in an intuitive way, by drawing on previous experience and vague, but not necessarily inaccurate notions of the complex relationships between market share and desirable aspects of company development.

If we compare with our model of the individual creative process empirical data investigation mostly resembles the latter part of the preparation period. The widening of the problem area no longer dominates, instead the reversed process of narrowing the focus, and concentrating on filling in gaps, is starting to gain in importance. This switch in perspective is crucial to success in the creative process, and the ability to do so constructively at the right time a major requirement for both individual and company creativity.

Building up an intuitive feeling for what types of data to collect may be viewed as the main purpose of the intuitive mode of company problem solving. Deciding when to stop widening and to start narrowing the analysis, that is when to enter the data investigation mode, also requires intuitive judgement. Intuition, thus, may be viewed as the main guiding principle in both these modes of company problem solving — as well as during early stages of the creative process — since the conditions for entering the data investigation mode also largely determines the way the continued narrowing process is carried out.

It is when applying the data investigation mode that computerized aids, for instance marketing information systems may be of greatest help by speeding up the collection and display of a wide variety of data. This requires, however, that the information systems are highly flexible and adaptive and permit decision makers to easily rearrange and recombine the data, to fit in with and help to develop their intuitive ideas.

To achieve such flexibility a disaggregated, detailed data bank and ready access to the basic data, are desirable (Arpi, 1970). The user of the information system can, then easily play around with the data, which as we remember from our discussion of the individual creative process is important for generating new ideas (insight).

Further assistance in the data investigation mode is possible by using explorative statistical techniques. Factor analysis, latent profile analysis, discriminant analysis and canonical analysis are examples of multivariate statistical methods, suited for this purpose (Aaker, 1971). By using such methods searching through vast quanties of data to find interesting data combinations is facilitated.

In contract to more conventional statistical techniques — such as chi-square tests — these explorative techniques are best suited for suggesting, rather than testing hypotheses. They, therefore, are most useful in the data investigation mode of problem solving, while conventional statistical techniques are most appropriate in the formal planning mode (see below). Verifying and checking, rather than formulating results, then, is the main concern, in analogy with the verification stage of the individual creative process.

For cost and time reasons — and because practical decision makers are often suspicious of analytical techniques — the use of sophisticated statistical techniques is, however, usually quite limited in all modes of problem solving in most companies. To some extent this suspicion may also be justified, as we have noted in our discussion of intuition versus analysis, as a basis for problem solving and decision making.

When using the data investigation mode it is important that decision makers have enough time and freedom for constructive thinking. We may compare with what we have said about the need for an incubation period in the individual creative process to facilitate insight. Financial security and a lack of pressure to immediately deal with problems may be seen as company factors encouraging and leading to psychological safety and freedom, which we emphasized before as important conditions for individual creativity.

In the data investigation mode richness in resources is therefore probably more essential to success than organizational flexibility, which we stressed when discussing the intuitive mode of decision making. Flexibility is necessary for setting the stage and stimulating informational richness. To use this wealth of information imaginatively, time and lack of conflicting claims to attention are, however, also necessary. Richness in resources, by increasing financial and psychological security, and giving decision makers better opportunity to reflect on new areas of action, should be of major importance in this connection.

Theoretical analysis

If problem specific, systematic data collection is difficult to carry out, or if for some reason the company does not feel it has time or money to carry out empirical data investigation, the company may go directly from the intuitive mode to the theoretical mode of problem solving. In this case the analytical basis

— the causal relationships — thus is explicit and systematic, while the empirical basis is implicit and intuitive, as in the case of intuitive problem solving.

The company in this instance tries to achieve a short cut and speed up the problem solving by applying general solutions to specific problems, without directly confronting empirical data. If the problems are well defined, and similiar problems have been successfully solved by the company before, favourable conditions will prevail for applying the theoretical mode. This makes this mode of problem solving particularly suited for positional companies, which by definition are working in stable problem solving environments. Experience may in this case be directly translated into general theoretical models, which can then be used as valuable guides in future problem solving.

To combine generality with clarity, simplicity is a desirable characteristic of theoretical analysis. Simple, concise models run the risk, however, of being bad approximations of any empirical conditions they are intended to represent. Linear relationships are, for instance, often assumed in theoretical models, not because they resemble actual conditions, but because they simplify the analysis. Since theoretical analysis, once started, tends to proceed along the lines drawn up, the risk of amplifying, rather than reducing initial errors, is great as we have noted before. For this reason theoretical analysis tends to be best suited at late stages of the creative process, when empirical focusing has taken place and it is a question of verifying, rather than exploring and formulating solutions.

In the case of well-defined problems and routine decision making, the empirical structuring of the problem area has taken place during previous attempts to solve similar problems, and as long as the conditions do not change, need not be repeated. If conditions do change, however, using theoretical analysis for the purpose of speeding up the problem solving will be a highly risky proposition.

We need to distinguish, therefore, between using theoretical analysis for summing up and verifying the implications of a specific instance of problem solving — which is always justified — and using it to generalize from previous experience — which is justified only if the problem solving situation has not changed.

Innovative companies probably will have more occasion to use theoretical analysis in the former sense of following up intuitive problem solving than positional companies, since their problem solving environments will tend to charge more over time. Positional companies, on the other hand, should have more occasion and reason to use theoretical analysis, in the sense of generalizing from previous experience, than innovative companies.

To be successful as a short cut to problem solving, theoretical analysis thus requires that problems be well defined from the start. The problem goals need to be clearly stated and the assumptions and functional relationships realistic and well adapted to the problem. In practice these requirements are often violated, and vague and badly understood problems are treated as if they were clear and well understood.

With regard to pricing, for instance, attempts are often made to apply the traditional single-product price model of economic theory to situations where the model is not applicable, and its underlying assumptions highly unrealistic. This is the case, for instance, with regard to retail pricing of convenience type goods, where an entirely different type of model is needed (Nyström, 1970). Another example, more in line with the discussion in this book, is long run planning, where models based on extrapolating linear trends are often used, even when it is clear that radical changes are taking place in the company and its environment.

The main problem in theoretical analysis thus is that realistic and comprehensive models tend not to have simple and clear-cut conclusions and are difficult to generalize across a wide range of situations. This problem has not received much attention in the management literature, although simulation models (Naylor and coworkers, 1966) have been proposed as a possible solution to this problem. Simulation implies a detailed theoretical structuring of the problem situation and working through the implications of the model by high speed calculation. Such, usually computer based, analysis has the advantage of a wide and detailed approach, but the disadvantage of making intuitive guidance and appraisal of the results difficult.

There is a need, thus, for theoretical models which are more detailed and complex than traditional analytical models, but more simple and therefore less confusing in their implications and results, than simulation models. These models would retain sufficient realism for intuitive acceptance by practical decision makers, yet be simple enough to avoid the disadvantages of carrying analytical complexity too far. Some attempts have been made to construct such models, for instance in the marketing area (Montgomery and Urban, 1970), but the need for further work along these lines is great.

A main problem in employing theoretical analysis, which follows from what has been said above, is that it requires that decision makers combine intuitive and analytical skills. Few individuals can operate at a high level in both modes, and, as we have noted before, being able to do so — and to switch constructively from one mode to another — is a main factor distinguishing between highly creative and less creative individuals.

Operating successfully in the theoretical mode of company problem solving thus demands that individuals also can operate in the intuitive mode and combine the two perspectives. This may well be another reason why theoretical analysis is used relatively little in actual company problem solving and decision making. It is then not only a question of avoiding the possible negative effects which formal analysis may have by restricting the flexibility of thought. It is also likely that few individuals are capable of combining intuition with formal analysis on a high level of performance. Relying mainly on intuitive individuals and intuition for *developing* solutions, may then be a less risky proposition for companies, than relying mainly on analytical individuals and analysis for the same purpose.

This, of course does not mean that formal analysis may not, and should not, be used for verifying solutions and for planning purposes, in other words to check on and coordinate efforts to realize the action agreed upon. Instead, this is probably the main use for formal analysis in actual company problem solving and decision making, as we shall see in the next section.

Formal planning

The final mode of company problem solving in our discussion is formal planning. Both the data basis and the causal relationships are then explicit and systematic, and the major problem solving effort involves coordinating company efforts to implement the proposed solutions (Mumford and Pettigrew, 1975). This, then, also implies verifying the solution with regard to its feasibility for achieving overall company goals.

The planning mode resembles the intuitive mode in emphasizing the overall perspective. In contrast to the data investigation mode and the theoretical mode it is aimed at building up the total picture, rather than breaking it down, in order to make possible specific data gathering or theoretical analysis of critical relationships.

On the other hand the planning mode is analytical in the sense that it makes necessary the expression of overall company objectives in formal, operational terms to make possible planning and budgeting procedures. In contrast to intuitive assessment, the conditions and requirements for problem solving need to be clearly stated at the start of the formal planning mode. In this sense, by demanding a clear statement of the tentative solution to the problem, it resembles the verification stage of the individual creative process, with its focus on clarity to make possible testing and communication of results.

As previously stated analytical precision tends, however, to lead to a delimitation of the problem solving area, which may be carried too far by analytically inclined individuals. In the formal planning mode there is thus a need not — as in the intuitive mode — to widen the initial perspective, but to maintain it, in spite of analytical pressure to narrow the scope.

To prevent such undesirable narrowing of the problem area during formal planning the company may employ various measures. It may, for instance, decentralize the planning process as much as possible so that many different people, representing different functions and areas of interest and competence, are involved. Greater central control of the problem solving should be exercised, however, than in the intuitive mode, since the objective is to maintain, not to widen the area of investigation.

Since a decentralized planning process takes a long time to carry out the company needs to keep a close eye on environmental conditions, so that changes do not occur which radically alter the empirical basis of the planning process. This type of checking is probably best carried out in the intuitive mode, by a decentralized process involving different types of people with good environmental contact, such as marketing or sales representatives. To coordinate their efforts a planning committee may be set up, with the purpose of determining if and when the conditions for formal planning have changed sufficiently to indicate the need for a different, more explorative mode of problem solving.

Flexibility in the planning mode need not imply, therefore, that the planning process itself is unformalized and intuitive. Instead, as we have seen, there is a need for coordination and control in this mode, which demands a relatively formal and directed approach to problem solving. Flexibility may instead be achieved by being sensitive to the need for activating other modes of problem solving, to provide a new set of conditions for the planning mode. This control, as we have noted above, may be carried out well in the intuitive mode. Intuition then plays a passive role, however, and becomes active in the problem solving process only when conditions have charged sufficiently to alter the basic premises of the planning process.

4.6 An integrated view of company problem solving

So far company creativity has been discussed against the background of the requirements of the individual creative process and company problem solving. The emphasis has been on how different factors, on the individual or company level, may affect the likelihood of success during different stages of the creative process and in different modes of company problem solving.

In practice, of course, the different activities are highly interrelated, may overlap in time and will not follow a strict sequential order. This is particularly the case with regard to the various modes of problem solving, since different types of problems and various environmental conditions will require differences in both the relative importance of different approaches to problem solving and in the time sequences in which they operate.

The suggested stages of the creative process and modes of company problem solving should be viewed, therefore, as discussion aids emphasizing important factors, rather than as accurate descriptions of necessary and sufficient conditions at different points of time.

Real companies, of course, are always characterized by both innovative and positional tendencies, and differ in their relative emphasis of one or the other, rather than in absolute terms, as being extreme instances of either category. Achieving a balance within the company — at any moment and over time — between factors favourable to either change or stability, then becomes the overall problem in establishing appropriate conditions for company creativity.

Following what we have said before rapid and discontinuous environmental change, by posing radically new problems, will require a strong initial emphasis on intuitive and exploratory problem solving. More routine problems in stable environments may be directly tackled, however, by theoretical analysis, if the company has previous experience of the problem area.

Innovative companies, therefore, should be more concerned with intuitive assessment and empirical data investigation, compared to positional companies, which should be more concerned with theoretical analysis and formal planning. Likewise innovative companies should be highly interested in recruiting and stimulating intuitive individuals, and individuals who can work in, and switch between, both intuitive and analytical patterns of thought. Positional companies, on the other hand, should be able to function well with more analytically oriented individuals, and intuition may be less necessary — or even disturbing — as long as their more stable problem solving situations persist.

It is, however, also necessary in all types of companies to achieve a balance between the need for innovative development and day-to-day operations. In positional companies the main preoccupation is with maintaining favourable conditions for day-to-day operations. As we have noted above, this means that the theoretical mode of problem solving becomes highly useful, and intuition and empirical data investigation less crucial to success.

In innovative companies, however, the problem of balancing different elements in the problem solving process becomes much more complicated. These companies need to maintain favourable conditions for both innovative development and day-to-day operations. As we have noted above these two types of activities pose quite different problems for company problem solving.

This creates an organizational need to separate problem solving for innovative development purposes, from routine problem solving for operational purposes. As we have noted before, innovative conditions calls for quite different, more intuitive and explorative problem solving during the initial phases, than routine problem solving. To successfully attack radically new problems we therefore, in accordance with our previous discussion, need a open and flexible, relatively unformalized organization structure and intuitively oriented individuals. To help to achieve this, companies may form separate development departments, such as new product or venture divisions, or employ a matrix organization, with R and D projects as one of the two dual structures.

Day-to-day operations may then be carried out in more formalized functional departments and divisions, or in the functionally specialized structure of a matrix organization, by employing more analytically oriented decision makers. The necessary coordination for planning purposes between the two types of activities may be achieved by informal contacts in a matrix organization, or by more formal integration mechanisms, such as committees or coordinating roles carried out by individuals or departments (compare Chapter 2).

Company creativity thus requires that the company carry out an intricate balancing act, requiring both organizational and psychological flexibility and formal planning and control, to differentiate between and integrate the changing requirements of the different stages of the creative process and different models of company problem solving.

4.7 Summary of Chapter 4

In this chapter company creativity is viewed against the background of what we know about individual creativity, and how these conditions may affect company problem solving. Individual creativity is regarded as a basic requirement for company creativity, and thus as indirectly responsible for successful innovation.

At the individual level the creative process may be divided into four stages. In practice it is difficult to distinguish them clearly from one another, but for discussion purposes the distinction is valuable. The first stage is the preparation period, the second the incubation period, the third the period of illumination or insight and the fourth the verification stage. The first three are mainly concerned to keep the problem open, while the last is chiefly concerned with its delimitation, that is with narrowing down the area of investigation.

Some of the personal attributes that favor the widening of the problem area are openness to experience, playfulness, ability to consider many possibilities and an intuitive way of thinking; problem delimitation on the other hand benefits from the ability to concentrate on certain aspects, a critical attitude and an analytical way of thinking. Furthermore, independence, a sense of psychological safety and freedom and an internal locus of evaluation are all factors which seem to promote creativity. Although there has been some controversy about this, most creativity researchers today seem to feel that there are fairly distinct differences between people as regards creative ability (regarded as a factor that is comparatively independent of general intelligence).

Group interaction can affect the relationship between individual and company creativity. In the present context I look on group interaction as a factor which — similarly to economic resources and company organization — may condition the degree of company creativity, but not primarily determine it. Group interaction can, for example be a positive factor particularly during the preparation stage. It can help to extend the individual's experience and it can allow for confrontations between different points of view. It can also aid the final verification stage by providing added control of the results. But during the critical intermediate stage, when new ideas are being born, it is the individual contributions that seem to be of decisive importance.

Group interaction can also affect the conditions of creativity on the motivational plane. It seems that a strong feeling of group cohesiveness — perhaps because the group is fairly homogeneous in certain respects relevant to the problem — enhances the members' sense of psychological safety and freedom and should therefore stimulate creativity. At the same time, though, plenty of variety in the group could also have a stimulating effect on creativity, just because it broadens the views and give the analysis a wider scope. Thus the total effect of the homogeneity or variety of the group on the creativity of its members is not clear.

When we turn directly to company creativity we may distinguish between different modes of company problem solving suitable under different conditions. Intuitive assessment refers to the case when both the data basis and causal relationships for understanding the data are implicit and intuitive. Empirical data investigation refers to the mode of problem solving when the data basis is explicit and systematic, but the causal relationships implicit and intuitive. Theoretical analysis is when the data basis is implicit and intuitive, but the causal relationship explicit and systematic, while formal planning finally refers to the mode of problem solving when both the data basis and the causal relationships are explicit and systematic.

When companies neither know what type of systematic data collection to use or how to analyse data, intuitive assessment is called for. This type of problem solving should be particularly important in innovative companies, and may sometimes even lead to final decisions, without using other modes of problem solving. This may even be in the company's best interest, since systematic data investigation is usually costly and time consuming, and theoretical analysis runs the risk of amplifying original errors in defining and formulating the problem.

If intuitive decision making does not take place empirical data investigation and/or theoretical analysis may be employed to empirically or theoretically narrow the problem solving area. Formal planning, finally, involves coordinating the overall efforts of the company to implement solutions and try to achieve intended results.

Positional companies may, against this background, be expected to be less interested in intuitive problem solving and empirical data investigation than innovative companies, and to make more use of theoretical analysis and formal planning.

The reason is that positional companies are better able to generalize from previous experience, due to greater stability in their problem solving situations, and this makes it easier for them to develop and apply theoretical analysis and less necessary for them to collect empirical data, to keep up with environmental change. Formal planning, then, may be based to a large extent on theoretical analysis, and should be of greater importance to positional than to innovative companies, since changes in the empirical data basis is less likely to rapidly invalidate the planning results.

A problem for innovative companies is balancing the different problem solving needs of innovative development and day-to-day operations. Positional companies may give priority to operational needs, but innovative companies must consider both in combination. This requires that development activities and ongoings operations be clearly separated in the organization and coordination be achieved by a dual organization structure (matrix organization) or other coordinating mechanisms such as committees.

In the case of both individual and company creativity the main problem, thus, is coordinating the demands for intuitive openness and analytical closure in working towards new solutions. The requirements for success will vary over the creative process, and between different modes of company problem solving. This is the problem facing companies when trying to achieve a clear innovative orientation. In Chapter 7 this problem will be further discussed when developing our integrated economic and psychological model of company development.

CHAPTER 5

Marketing Strategy and Company Development

5.1 Introduction

Many attempts have been made to arrive at basic classifications of marketing strategies since Chamberlin around 1930, by introducing imperfect competition, made it theoretically possible to consider marketing as an active component in company behaviour (Chamberlin, 1933). These classification schemes have been directed to the question what type of marketing companies should carry out in various market and demand situations.

Most suggested classifications in the literature have, however, serious limitations. Due to the fact that they are based on traditional economic thinking, they are for instance basically static in their implications. By utilizing such classifications it becomes possible for companies to consider existing *differences* in buyer demand and competition for given markets, but it is much more difficult to use them to consider *changes* over time in market conditions. In addition these classifications are analytically tied to single products, which makes them difficult to apply to the study of complex, multiproduct companies.

The purpose of this chapter is mainly to discuss how positional and innovative companies ideally should design their marketing strategies. Positional companies, by definition, are concerned with maintaining and utilizing existing conditions. Their company environment is stable and simple to promote efficiency through standardization, specialization and economics of scale. From a marketing point of view this is made possible by a small number of established products, with long life cycles and stable demand. If such conditions prevail, traditional classifications of marketing strategies, derived from static competition theory, are relatively applicable.

With regard to innovative companies, however, the ideal company environment is highly complex and changing. The innovative orientations of these companies, and dynamic nature of their appropriate markets, will in general lead to a high rate of product change and many new products in their offerings. To analyse their marketing strategies we thus need a dynamic classification of marketing situations, which considers total company behaviour in an extended time perspective.

To begin with we will first discuss two classification schemes in the economic tradition. These schemes are single-product oriented, and therefore difficult to apply to the total marketing situation of multiproduct companies, even under stable conditions. A dynamic classification (Nyström, 1972a, 1972b) will be proposed as an alternative approach, better suited for analysing the marketing strategies of companies working under complex and changing conditions. This classification distinguishes between more open and more closed marketing strategies and focuses on total market relationships, rather than isolated demand for single products.

In addition to being better suited to analysing the marketing situation of innovative companies, than traditional classifications, this approach makes it possible to compare both the ideal and actual marketing strategies of positional and innovative companies. The suggested classification represents a scale from highly open and flexible strategies — suitable for innovative companies in changing environments — to highly closed and restricted strategies — well adapted to the needs of positional companies in stable environments. As in the case of our basic company classification model, we thus achieve an ideal classification, which fits into and extends our general analysis in Chapter 2 of company development under different environmental conditions.

5.2 Product differentiation versus market segmentation

A commonly used classification of basic marketing strategies is *product differentiation* versus *market segmentation* (Smith, 1956; Mathiesen, 1971). This distinction is based on the theory of imperfect competition, and signifies that a company can either influence or adapt to market complexity, by changing customer demand or by concentrating on more uniform segments of the market. Compared to perfect competition, where homogeneity is assumed both with regard to supply and demand, the more realistic assumption thus is made that buyer preferences and the products of competing companies are differentiated.

On such markets companies can either chose product differentiation (Chamberlin, 1962) — i.e. try to increase the relative attractiveness of their product — or market segmentation (Arndt, 1974) — i.e. concentrate on market segments where their product is superior to other products. In the first instance the company tries to make total market demand more uniform — in the sense that more buyers will prefer its product. In the second instance the company tries to take advantage of the existing differences in demand.

Both these strategies are essentially static, by not considering changes in market conditions unless they are the result of the company's own activities. Therefore this type of market classification is most useful under relatively stable market conditions, compared to situations where demand changes rapidly over time. Since the analysis is based on single products, it is also best suited for companies where one product dominates, or where cost and demand interdependencies between products are unimportant. The analysis also assumes that only product modifications, that is marginal product changes, take place. This is both a methodological weakness, since it is difficult to draw the line between product modifications and new products, and a serious limitation, since new products are excluded from the analysis.

The analytical limitations of the classification thus makes the distinction between product differentiation and market segmentation mainly of interest in analysing the marketing strategies of positional companies. Their marketing situation ideally is characterized by stable and simple conditions, which makes this type of analysis quite realistic. In the case of innovative companies the analysis is inadequate to reflect the complex and changing nature of their ideal marketing situation.

5.3 Undifferentiated, differentiated and concentrated marketing

Another classification of marketing strategies, which also is closely related to competition theory, has been proposed by Kotler (1967). In this case a distinction is made between *undifferentiated, differentiated* and *concentrated marketing*. The basis is a division of the market into segments. Undifferentiated marketing means that the same product is sold everywhere without differences in marketing mix and intensity between segments. Differentiated marketing that the product and/or marketing mix is adapted to the conditions prevailing in each segment and concentrated marketing that only the most profitable segments are dealt with.

This classification is intuitively attractive and more comprehensive than the above related classification, which only distinguishes between two strategies, product differentiation and market segmentation. At the same time it is difficult to apply consistently to data since it — similar to other classification schemes based on economic theory — relies on achieving a clear picture of the total market. In practice, markets are difficult to isolate and, depending on whether we use a wide or narrow market definition, we may well arrive at different conclusions as to whether the marketing strategy of a company is undifferentiated, differentiated or concentrated. This, in particular, makes it difficult to compare the marketing strategies of companies operating in different markets by employing this type of classification. It is less serious when we want to consider changes in the marketing strategy of a given company.

Basically the limits of Kotler's classification are the same as for the classification based on product differentiation and market segmentation. It is static and single-product oriented, which makes it mainly applicable to studying the marketing strategies of positional companies. Due to its basic assumptions it is not well suited for analysing the marketing strategies of innovative companies, or for marketing comparisons between positional and innovative companies.

5.4 The need for a dynamic classification of marketing strategies

Based on the previous discussion there appears to be a need for a classification of marketing strategies which is dynamic, that is considers changes over time in marketing conditions. As noted above, most existing classifications may be used by a company to differentiate their marketing strategies along the static dimension and thereby adapt to existing differences between market segments. It is not, however, possible to use this type of static classification to consider changes over time, that is to make possible a differentiation also along the time dimension. With regard to positional companies working in stable environments adapting to existing differences in market conditions is the main problem. Static classifications of marketing situations may then be quite sufficient. With regard to innovative companies working under complex and changing market conditions static classifications by definition are inadequate and dynamic classifications instead necessary.

The purpose of the proposed classification of marketing strategy as more open or closed — presented in the following section — is to consider both static and dynamic aspects of marketing strategy, that is both established relationships and radical change. This makes necessary a more total view of company development than traditional single-product models make possible. The addition of new products or substitution of new products for old ones is impossible to analyse in a single-product framework. By focusing on buyer relationships, rather than products, a more total and comprehensive approach to studying marketing strategies will be proposed. Within this framework both product modifications and new products may be considered in a dynamic context.

5.5 Open and closed marketing strategies

The basis of the suggested approach to marketing is how *open* or *closed* the marketing strategy of a company is. The fewer buyers a company has and the more stable buyer relationships are, the more closed, i.e. narrow and restricted, its orientation is. The larger the number of customers and the greater the variability in customer relationships, the more open, i.e. wide and flexible, its strategy is. We may in theory distinguish between two extreme cases with regard to market orientation. The first, which we may call *a completely closed marketing strategy*, involves one buyer, identically the same over time. The second, which we may call *a completely open marketing strategy*, involves an infinitely large number of buyers, with continuously changing identities, that is new buyers constantly replacing old ones. These two cases, especially the second one, are of course theoretical points of reference in relation to which more realistic market orientations may be seen, rather than empirically interesting descriptions of actual situations. In this respect their function for our analysis is the same as the theoretical distinction between positional and innovative companies.

This classification of marketing strategy considers both the static spatial dimension of market demand-emphasized in economic theory — and the dynamic time dimension, necessary to study in an innovative theory of the firm. The former is reflected in the number of buyers at any point of time and the latter in their variability over time. Both these dimensions are of fundamental importance for analysing and understanding marketing strategies, and therefore are considered in our classification.

Instead of directly relating marketing efforts to the sales of individual products — as in traditional economic models — our approach is based on how marketing affects the total structure of buyer relationships of a company. Only if marketing efforts — for instance price and quality changes — lead to changes in these buyer relationships, as defined above, will they therefore influence the classification of the marketing strategy in our analysis.

There will, for instance, be no direct, necessary relationship between product differentiation as a marketing strategy and our concept of open or closed marketing strategy. Product differentiation, as noted above, primarily is concerned with making existing customers more loyal to the offering of a company. In the short run product differentiation need not, therefore, affect how open or closed the marketing strategy of a company is, since the number and identity of customers is given, and it is merely a question of tying these customers closer to the company. In the long run, however, product differentiation may conceivably often, but not automatically, lead to a more closed marketing strategy for a company, by contributing to more stable buyer relationships.

Similarly, there will be no direct, general relationship between market segmentation and how open or closed the marketing strategy of a company is. By focusing on stable and narrow segments of the market, a company may, however, achieve a more closed marketing strategy, and by focusing on more wide and changeable segments a more open strategy. By making product differentiation easier, concentrated marketing may for instance lead to a more closed marketing strategy, than differentiated or undifferentiated marketing, but this, then, is an indirect and highly uncertain relationship.

Product innovations, radically new products, may be expected to lead to more open and flexible marketing strategies in most instances, by appealing to new customer groups.

Product modifications, on the other hand, usually appeal to the same customers as the original products, and therefore should be less likely to lead to open marketing strategies, than new products. Since positional companies may be expected to emphasize product modifications and innovative companies new products, this means that our classification of marketing strategy should be suited for analysing differences between these types of companies.

5.6 Selective and non-selective marketing techniques

The marketing strategy of a company — measured by how open or closed it is — depends on both the marketing techniques of the company and environmental factors beyond its control.

With regard to marketing techniques we may for our purpose distinguish between *selective* and *non-selective techniques*. Selective marketing techniques are directed towards and adapted to specific individual customers. Non-selective techniques, on the other hand, are intended to stimulate more total market demand, without focusing on individual customers. Examples of selective marketing techniques are personal selling and direct advertising, while mass media advertising and sales promotion, are examples of non-selective marketing techniques.

We may assume that there is a relatively clear empirical relationship between selective or non-selective marketing techniques on the one hand and open or closed marketing strategy on the other. It should be possible for companies to achieve more closed marketing strategies in most instances by using selective marketing techniques.

But at the same time the marketing environment of a company sets a limit to how far a company can and should try to make its marketing strategy more open or closed.

To maintain and strengthen simple and stable environments — beneficial to achieving short run efficiency through planning and control — positional companies should usually find it to their advantage to try to achieve closed marketing strategies by employing selective marketing techniques. This means focusing their efforts on those segments of the market which promise lasting rewards without making necessary radical changes in the company's line and way of doing business.

Innovative companies, on the other hand, thrive on complexity and change. This leads to, and makes necessary more open, wide and flexible marketing strategies, to take advantage of the possibilities which arise. Non-selective marketing techniques — appealing to wide segments of the market — should help to create and maintain such orientations in changing environments. In such instances the company does not know in advance exactly what customers to focus on. Non-selective marketing techniques are in tune with this, by searching for and helping to establish new buyer relationships.

5.7 A comparison with competition theory

Our approach, in contrast to traditional economic analysis based on competition theory (Henderson and Quandt, 1958) is not directly related to products. Instead, as we have seen, it is based on the total structure of buyer relationships, to make possible a more comprehensive and dynamic view of company marketing. To facilitate comparisons between our view and more traditional approaches, an attempt will be made below to compare and discuss them in relation to each other.

In this connection it is helpful to distinguish between two types of products. *Specialized products* are products with few possible uses, that is with a narrow area of application. *General products* are products with many different uses, actual and potential.

As an example of highly specialized products we may take special machinery, while raw material, such as chemicals, are an example of more general products.

This product-based distinction may be composed to a customer-based distinction, centering on differences in the structure of buyer relationships. The customer structure of a company may be more or less *concentrated* or *non-concentrated*, with regard to the number, size or geographical location of customers. Smaller number, larger average sales per customer and geographically denser location then imply greater concentration.

The following hypotheses may now be formulated with regard to the relationship between our buyer-related approach to marketing strategy and other product-based approaches, based on competition theory.

1. Specialized product type and a concentrated, actual customer structure makes it desirable for companies to try to achieve a relatively closed marketing strategy by employing selective marketing techniques. This combination of product type and customer structure also should make it relatively easy for companies to succeed in this respect. If existing and potential customers largely are the same in an extended time perspective, the tendencies will be strengthened. If product changes are few and marginal, and buyer preferences are stable over time, this type of product–buyer situation is an ideal one for positional companies. The limiting, extreme case is a stable situation of bilateral monopoly, with one buyer and one seller confronting each other. Negotiations between the two parties will then be the main ingredient in a highly focused and very selective approach to marketing.

2. Specialized product type and a non-concentrated actual buyer structure, means that a closed marketing strategy is desirable from the company's point of view, at least in the short run. This type of orientation will be difficult for the company to achieve, however, in an economically satisfactory way. In practice, therefore, companies in this situation may be forced to choose more non-selective marketing techniques, than companies in the first case, with specialized product type and a concentrated, actual buyer structure. If the potential buyer structure differs greatly from the actual one, the necessity and possibility of successfully achieving an open marketing strategy in the long run will be greater, due to the market opportunity for change. Product differentiation — marginal product changes to achieve a better balance between product characteristics and attractive segments of market demand — will be immediately attractive to the company in this instance. If buyer preferences are changing rapidly and the innovative potential of the company is sufficient, product innovation, however, may be a better choice to the company in the long run, than product modification. The marketing situations of companies becoming innovative, as a response to environmental change, may characteristically show this type of product–buyer relation. In a static perspective this situation resembles imperfect competition with product differentiation in competition theory. For our purpose, however, the long run aspects of the situation are of greater interest, and to analyse them we need a different, more dynamic approach.

3. General product type and a concentrated actual buyer structure, means that a closed marketing strategy is less necessary than in the second case. This is because of the likelihood of finding new customers when old ones disappear. At the same time the company already has a closed strategy in a static perspective, as shown by its concentrated buyer structure. It may be changing, however, towards a more open marketing strategy, since this is in line with the characteristics of the product. By employing non-selective marketing techniques, the company may facilitate such a change in market orientation, if it wants to. In this case product changes will probably be less necessary because of

the possibility of finding new customers for the existing product, and less easy to carry out, because of the general nature of the product. From a product development point of view the situation will most likely be characterized by positional tendencies, because of difficulties in technically developing the product. From a buyer selection point of view innovative tendencies may, however, be quite strong, due to the favourable possibilities for finding new customers. This product–buyer situation resembles imperfect competition, without product differentiation, in competition theory.

4. General product type and a non-concentrated acutal buyer structure means that an open marketing strategy is called for, and non-selective marketing techniques suitable for achieving this. If demand is stable and product changes infrequent, active marketing will, however, be by and large unnecessary. Passive marketing — merely making the product available to distributors and consumers — will be emphasized instead. If demand is changeable and product changes more frequent the product–buyer situation, for competitive reasons, may be expected to change, instead, to a specialized product type and/or concentrated buyer structure. This, then, turns this case into one of the other cases. In its extreme version this case resembles pure competition in economic theory, which rules out product changes and active marketing.

5.8 Summary of Chapter 5

In this chapter I suggest a basic classification of company marketing strategies, based on how open or closed they are. The basis for this classification is the number of customers and the variability of buyer relationships over time. The fewer a company's customers and the more stable its buyer relationships, the more closed — narrow and restricted — its strategy is. The greater the number of customers and the more unstable the relationships, the more open — wide and flexible — is the strategy.

Thus, viewed in these terms, the company's marketing strategy is a function of its own action and of other factors over which the company has no control. This means that by applying selective marketing techniques — personal selling, direct advertising and so on — the company can achieve a more closed marketing strategy. By applying non-selective techniques, on the other hand, e.g. mass media advertising, it can develop a more open marketing strategy.

Unlike the more traditional classifications of marketing strategy (product differentiation versus market segmentation for example) the classification suggested here is based on the company's total operations, rather than on individual products. Moreover it allows for the dynamic element in the market situation as well as the static.

To be able to enjoy the advantages of scale and the benefits of planning and specialization, the positional company operating in the kind of stable and simple market environment that suits it, should aim at a more closed, narrow and restricted, marketing strategy, perhaps by employing selective marketing techniques. Innovative companies in changeable, complex and therefore uncertain environments, on the other hand, should aim at a more open, wide and flexible, marketing strategy, perhaps by applying more non-selective, general marketing techniques.

The chapter concludes with an attempt to relate this dynamic approach based on customer relationships to the static, product-based approach of competition theory. By classifying products as general and specialized and customer structure as concentrated and non-concentrated, it is possible to draw parallels with different competitive environments — monopoly, imperfect competition and pure competition. In light of the argument presented in this chapter it is then possible to suggest which traditional type of competition and which traditional market situation that suits the innovative and positional company respectively.

CHAPTER 6

Company Strategies for Research and Development: an Empirical Application

6.1 Introduction

In this chapter a specific application of our proposed theoretical framework to an important aspect of company development, company strategies for R and D, will be presented. In spite of the importance of this problem area, both from a societal and from a company management point of view, few empirical studies of overall company R and D strategies have been reported in the literature.

Most research (e.g. Mansfield, 1968; Marquis and Myers, 1969; Achilladeles, Jervis and Robertson, 1971; Jewkes, Sawers and Stillerman, 1958), has been directed, instead, towards analysing the idea generation, marketing situation and technological background of new products in a product-specific, rather than company-related perspective. Differences between products, rather than between companies, have been emphasized. The overall strategic question of how companies directly or indirectly chose new markets and new areas of technology and organize and focus their research efforts, has so far received little attention in studies of product innovation.

Our main interest is in company, rather than product development. Studies of product innovation, which do not consider strategic and structural differences between companies, but merely product related differences, are therefore of interest to us, but too limited in their scope to provide a sufficient background for our analysis. Our approach starts, instead, with a general, overall conceptualization of R and D, and uses both policy statements and data for a number of individual products to give empirical content to the R and D strategy of a company. Product change thus is the main and crucial outcome of R and D in our analysis, but to understand such change we need to begin with a wider study of the overall conditions for company creativity and innovation.

Applying our theoretical framework positional and innovative companies may be expected to employ different R and D strategies. These strategies reflect different technological and market orientations in developing new products, and differences in the internal and external organization of R and D (Mansfield, 1968; Freeman, 1974; Gold, 1975; Roberts, 1976).

To begin with it is necessary to distinguish between *intended* and *realized* *strategies*. Intended strategies are expressed in explicit policy relating to R and

D activities, while realized strategies refer to consistent patterns of behaviour, which may or may not be the result of implementing policy decisions. Our primary concern is with realized strategies, but we also need to study intended strategies as a guide to what type of realized action to look for and as a basis for assessing and possibly changing R and D policy and policy implementation, if the intended action does not result, or leads to undesirable consequences.

In the present study intended strategies, that is R and D policy, is assessed from interview data on company policy and from company documents. This data is of a qualitative nature, difficult to analyse, but has wide applicability, since it refers to overall dimensions of company behaviour.

Realized strategies, on the other hand, are mainly inferred from data directly relating to individual products. This data is more detailed and easier to quantify than general policy statements, but also more difficult to use as an indication of overall company strategy. The interplay between different levels of analysis and different types of data (Glaser and Strauss, 1967) should tend to give a richer and more suggestive picture of R and D strategies, than would be possible with a more limited approach emphasizing one type of data. At the same time it permits systematic analysis of strategic differences between firms which is our objective.

6.2 Data collection

The empirical analysis in this chapter is based on in-depth interviews with about 30 representatives for 11 Swedish companies, carried out in late 1975 and early 1976, and on supplementary written material such as company documents and published reports, collected in connection with and after the interviews (Nyström, 1977). Three of the companies were in pharmaceuticals, two were steel companies, four were in electronics and two were non-pharmaceutical chemical companies.

In addition to general background data, and data on company policy and activities related to research and development, specific information was collected for 91 new products. These products were given as representative of the new products introduced by each of the companies during recent years. Both radically new products and product modifications, but not minor variations, were thus included, in proportions which reflected the emphasis which companies had given to each of these in their product development.

The more stable over time a company's R and D policy and its organization and direction of R and D appeared to have been, the more acceptable older products were judged to be, as representative of present day conditions. Of the 91 products, eight were introduced on the market before 1960, 27 between 1960 and 1970, 49 products after 1970, while seven products had not yet been introduced at the time of the interviews. In the case of the latter products market introduction was shortly to take place, and it was possible to estimate the factors of interest to our analysis.

6.3 R and D policy

Based on the interviews three main policy dimensions evolved (Table 6.1). The first we will call *concentrated* versus *diversified R and D*. This refers to the extent to which companies express a desire to branch out into new product areas and new areas of technology. If companies mainly wish to concentrate within their established areas we will call this a concentrated policy. If they want to enter new areas we will speak of a diversified policy.

We see that six of the companies studied emphasize diversification and five concentration. The differences are mainly between industries, with all pharmaceutical and chemical companies expressing a diversification policy and most of the steel and electronic companies stressing concentration (five of six). These policy differences thus seem to be more related to general market and technological conditions facing industries, than to company-specific differences, such as size, growth rate and internal organization. Within each

Table 6.1. R and D Policies in Different Companies

Company		Rand D policy		Policy classification
P.1	Diversified (1)	Technologically oriented (1)	Offensive (1)	Highly innovative (3)
P.2	Diversified (1)	Technologically oriented (1)	Offensive (1)	Highly innovative (3)
P.3	Diversified (1)	Technologically oriented (1)	Offensive (1)	Highly innovative (3)
S.1	Concentrated (0)	Technologically oriented (1)	Offensive (1)	Relatively innovative (2)
S.2	Concentrated (0)	Market oriented (0)	Defensive (0)	Highly positional (0)
E.1	Diversified (1)	Market oriented (0)	Defensive (0)	Relatively positional (1)
E.2	Concentrated (0)	Market oriented (0)	Offensive (1)	Relatively positional (1)
E.3	Concentrated (0)	Market oriented (0)	Offensive (1)	Relatively positional (1)
E.4	Concentrated (0)	Technologically oriented (1)	Offensive (1)	Relatively innovative (2)
C.1	Diversified (1)	Technologically oriented (1)	Offensive (1)	Highly innovative (3)
C.2	Diversified (1)	Market oriented (0)	Offensive (1)	Relatively innovative (2)

Higher numbers indicate a more innovative policy.

P.1, P.2, P.3 Pharmaceutical companies
S.1, S.2 Steel companies
E.1, E.2, E.3, E.4 Electronic companies
C.1, C.2 Chemical companies

industry we find differences along these lines, which do not appear to be related to policy differences in concentration versus diversification.

The second policy dimension concerns *technological* versus *market orientation* in seeking ideas for new products. Technologically oriented companies search for product ideas based on new technical principles, for instance discovered in university research or fundamental laboratory work. They then try to assess the market possibilities of the envisaged products. Market oriented companies first search for and specify unfulfilled user needs and then determine whether they have the technological means for designing products to satisfy these needs.

In this case the policy differences are less clearly related to industry. The pharmaceutical companies all have a technologically oriented policy, emphasizing technological leadership in narrow, advanced areas of technology. The electronic companies are mainly market oriented, stressing the combining and adaptation of known techniques and standard components to closely defined market specifications. The exception is a small, newly founded company pioneering in a new area of technology. In the steel and chemical companies, on the other hand, the policy differences seem to be more company than industry related. One of the steel companies has a relatively technologically oriented policy, emphasizing new materials and techniques and searching for new market applications. The other has a much more market oriented policy, trying to develop new products to fit clearly specified market needs. With regard to the chemical companies, one has a quite technologically oriented policy and is willing to develop technically interesting ideas, even when there is almost total uncertainty as to market demand. The other is basically market oriented in its policy, but its emphasis is changing in the direction of a more technological orientation.

The third policy dimension is *defensive* versus *offensive R and D*. A defensive policy implies that a company primarily wants to protect its established market and technological position, by developing and introducing new products mainly as a response to competitors trying to take business away from it. An offensive policy means that a company constantly wants to be ahead of competitors in new product development.

With regard to this policy dimension most companies emphasize the offensive use of R and D. One of the electronic companies and one of the steel companies, however, stress the basically defensive nature of their R and D. Both these companies are market oriented in their R and D and view following up customer needs as more important than checking on competitors with regard to their product development. Both try to tie customers to their products by joint R and D ventures, which if successful create a high degree of market protection and lessen the need for offensive R and D. The defensive electronic company emphasizes this aspect by essentially specializing in systems of custom-made equipment, utilizing standard components and close cooperation and integration of research with customers.

This type of research orientation does not, however, preclude offensive R and

D. Two of the other electronic companies and one of the chemical companies employ close customer cooperation in research together with an offensive policy. The pharmaceutical companies all view an offensive R and D policy as essential for survival, as does the second, offensive steel company. The first chemical company uses its offensive policy together with its technical orientation mainly to achieve product diversification. Before starting to diversify it had a basically defensive policy. On the other hand it is also possible to use an offensive and concentrated R and D policy, as the offensive steel company and two of the electronic companies show.

If we look at overall R and D policy some patterns emerge from the data. Diversified companies, for instance, tend to be technologically oriented and vice versa. Diversified and technologically oriented companies are also offensive in most instances, but since only two companies have a defensive policy, a number of offensive companies are concentrated and market oriented. The two defensive companies are both market oriented, but one has a concentrated and the other a diversified policy.

In order to analyse these overall patterns, our analytical distinction between innovative and positional companies will be employed. As defined in Chapter 2 innovative companies are companies which want to take advantage of new opportunities for company development, that tend to occur in environments characterized by rapid and radical changes. Positional companies, on the other hand, mainly try to maintain and strengthen their established positions, which is easiest to do in stable environments, with slow and continuous changes. These categories, of course, as we have noted before, are ideal constructions which are used in our analysis to highlight tendencies which are more or less pronounced in actual company behaviour.

In the analysis in this chapter of R and D strategies we will use diversification, technological orientation and offensiveness as indications of an open innovative R and D policy, while concentration, market orientation and a defensive policy will be used as indications of a closed positional policy. With regard to diversification and offensiveness the reasoning behind this procedure should be apparent since both imply aiming at product areas new to a company and being ahead of competitors in developing and introducing new products. In the case of technological versus market orientation, however, the reasoning is less straightforward, but nevertheless follows from the special sense in which the term technological orientation is used.

As noted above, technological orientation refers to a company being sensitive to new technical ideas and principles as possible avenues to new products, *before* any specific market applications are evident. Market orientation, on the other hand, implies that a company usually is not interested in developing new product ideas, unless they are firmly anchored in existing, percieved market needs. A technological orientation does not mean that market conditions are ignored. But it does mean that a company instead of primarily reacting to specific signals from the market, for instance to market research or customer reactions, tries to exploit technological possibilities for finding new products, when future demand may only be vaguely visualized, and perhaps also needs to be actively created by the company.

In the case of technological orientation, market possibilities thus are a more open question at the start of the formal R and D process, than in the case of market orientation. We may therefore say — with the definitions used — that technological orientation in R and D policy implies a more open and innovative R and D policy than market orientation.

If we look at Table 6.1 we find the most open and innovative R and D policies in the pharmaceutical and chemical companies and the most closed and positional among the steel and electronic companies. At the same time one of the steel companies and one of the chemical companies has a relatively innovative policy. To prevent misunderstanding, it must be stressed that the terms innovative or positional are not used to indicate desirable or non-desirable features of R and D policy, either from a company or societal point of view. Instead, depending on the internal and external environment of a company, either may be desirable, as a guide to successful R and D.

6.4 Realized R and D strategies

Similar to R and D policies, realized R and D strategies are measured along three dimensions. The first dimension is *orientation*, which may be more or less *external* or *internal*. Internally oriented companies emphasize internal competence and their own experts, when developing new products. Externally oriented companies, on the other hand, rely to a large extent on external consultants in carrying out R and D activities. Orientation is measured both with regard to idea generation and technical product development. In the first respect the question is whether the idea for a product has originated inside or outside a company. In the second respect we are interested in whether a company utilizes substantial outside help in developing a product idea or basically develops the idea on its own (joint or internal development).

From Table 6.2 we see that differences in orientation more reflect differences between companies than industries. Two of the three pharmaceutical companies, however, are quite externally oriented, while both steel companies show a strong internal orientation. There would appear to be some connection between company size and orientation. The largest pharmaceutical company, for instance is internally oriented, and the largest electronic company is much more internally oriented than the other electronic companies. Even large companies, however, may well need an external orientation to keep up with rapid technological change or to diversify. The first larger chemical company, for instance, is more externally oriented than the second smaller one. Small companies, on the other hand, by specializing in narrow areas of technology may successfully maintain a highly internal orientation, which is brought out in our data by the second electronic company and the second chemical company. For all companies combined, internal orientation is stronger than external

Table 6.2. Company Classification with Regard to External or Internal Orientation based on Number of Products in Different Categories

Company	Idea generation		Technical product development		Company classification
	External	Internal	Joint	Internal	
P.1	8	1	7	2	Highly external
P.2	3	7	3	7	Relatively internal
P.3	4	1	2	3	Relatively external
S.1	3	12	2	13	Highly internal
S.2	0	8	2	6	Highly internal
E.1	2	10	1	11	Highly internal
E.2	2	7	5	4	Relatively internal
E.3	2	4	2	4	Relatively internal
E.4	4	0	4	0	Highly external
C.1	5	3	6	2	Relatively external
C.2	2	3	2	3	Relatively internal
Total	35	56	36	55	

orientation, with 56 of the 91 products showing internal orientation in idea development and 55 in product development.

The second dimension of realized strategy is *technology use*. Companies, the new products of which are mainly the result of utilizing a single technology — e.g. biochemistry — are said to emphasize *isolated use of technology*. Companies, the new products of which are basically a result of combining different technologies — e.g. biochemistry and immunology — are said to emphasize *synergistic use of technology* (Table 6.3). Technologies are viewed as specialized areas of knowledge — usually separate areas of study at universities — which define and delimit the areas of interest and competence of most researchers. By requiring special, as opposed to general, knowledge of the literature, special research instruments and technical facilities and other types of specialization, established technologies represent barriers to interdisciplinary research, which must be overcome by companies engaging in synergistic use of technology.

In Table 6.4 we see that of the 11 companies, four are classified as using technology mainly in an isolated way, by deepening their competence in established areas of competence. Two are classified as making strong synergistic

Table 6.3. Examples of Isolated versus Synergistic use of Technology from the data

Isolated use of technology	Synergistic use of technology
Polymer technology	Biochemistry
	+
Immunology	Immunology
Biochemistry	Peripheral bloodflow
	+
Peripheral bloodflow	Polymer technology
	+
Microbiology	Immunology
Pharmachology	Microbiology
	+
Organic chemistry	Pharmachology
	+
Bacteriology	Bacteriology
Steel metallurgy	Steel metallurgy
	+
Welding technology	Welding technology
Hydromechanics	Biochemistry
	+
Fine mechanics	Optical measurement
	+
Optical measurement	Microelectronics
Microelectronics	Hydromechanics
	+
Powder metallurgy	Fine mechanics
	+
	Polymer technology
	Polymer technology
	+
	Powder metallurgy

use of technology, combining elements from different areas of technology to find new products. The remaining five companies have been classified as isolated/synergistic, which means that approximately half the products are classified as representing either type of technology use. In contrast to external/internal orientation a large number of companies thus tend to employ a mixed strategy of technology use, giving about equal emphasis to both aspects.

If we look at industries, the main difference is between the steel companies, who make strong isolated use of technology, and the other companies, who are more divided between an isolated and a synergistic use. If we except the newly

Table 6.4. Company Classification with Regard to Technology Use, Based on Number of Products where Technology Use is Isolated or Synergistic

Company	Technology use		Company classification
	Isolated	Synergistic	
P.1	4	5	Isolated/synergistic
P.2	9	1	Isolated
P.3	3	2	Isolated/synergistic
S.1	14	1	Isolated
S.2	6	2	Isolated
E.1	4	8	Synergistic
E.2	5	4	Isolated/synergistic
E.3	2	4	Synergistic
E.4	4	0	Isolated
C.1	4	4	Isolated/synergistic
C.2	3	2	Isolated/synergistic
Total	58	33	

formed electronic company, which makes isolated use of one new technology, the electronic companies, however, appear to be most synergistic. This probably reflects the highly competitive nature of research in electronics, with a resulting need to look beyond pure electronics to find unexploited market niches. There does not seem to be any clear connection between company size and isolated versus synergistic use of technology. The largest pharmaceutical company, for instance, shows a strong isolated use of technology, while the largest electronic company shows a synergistic use. For all companies combined, isolated use of technology, represented by 58 products, is more common than synergistic use, represented by 33 products.

The third dimension of realized R and D strategies is *fixed* versus *responsive organization* of R and D. In order to study this aspect of R and D, we must make use of general interview data, not related to individual products. Companies usually do not vary their internal organization of R and D to fit the needs of different products. Instead they normally employ a common approach to organizing R and D within the company. Variations between companies, however, are much more striking and may be related to differences in R and D strategies of interest to our study. In the following, three aspects of R and D organization will be distinguished between and an overall classification attempted by summarizing the three types of data (Table 6.5).

The first aspect is the organization of the company's *external information and contact network*. This has been classified as wide or narrow depending on how extensively the company searches in its external environment for ideas and outside cooperation in R and D. Some companies, for instance, search widely for ideas and assistance from customers, universities and consultants, and use

Table 6.5. Company Classification with Regard to External and Internal Organization of Research and Development

Com-pany	External information and contact network	Idea and project evaluation	Internal project work	Overall classification of a company organization of R and D
P.1	Wide and flexible (2)	Decentralized and informal (2)	Flexible project groups (1)	Highly responsive (5)
P.2	Wide and directed (1)	Centralized and formal (0)	Flexible project groups (1)	Relatively fixed (2)
P.3	Wide and flexible (2)	Decentralized and formal (1)	Flexible project groups (1)	Relatively responsive (4)
S.1	Narrow and directed (0)	Centralized and formal (0)	Fixed project groups (0)	Highly fixed (0)
S.2	Wide and directed (1)	Centralized and formal (0)	Fixed project groups (0)	Relatively fixed (1)
E.1	Wide and directed (1)	Decentralized and formal (1)	Fixed project groups (0)	Relatively fixed (2)
E.2	Wide and directed (1)	Centralized and informal (1)	Fixed project groups (0)	Relatively fixed (2)
E.3	Narrow and directed (0)	Decentralized and formal (1)	Fixed project groups (0)	Relatively fixed (1)
E.4	Narrow and directed (0)	Centralized and formal (0)	Fixed project groups (0)	Highly fixed (0)
C.1	Wide and flexible (2)	Decentralized and informal (2)	Flexible project groups (1)	Highly responsive (5)
C.2	Wide and directed (1)	Centralized and informal (1)	Flexible project groups (1)	Relatively responsive (3)

Higher numbers indicate a more responsive organization.

many different channels to reach these sources. Other companies have a more narrow focus, for instance mainly relying on customers as a source of new ideas and an aid in developing them. In addition to this, external contacts may be more or less flexible, depending on whether the company basically uses established channels and a given group of contacts, or varies its information and contact network depending on the circumstances. The least flexible organizations in our study employ fixed reference groups and search areas while the most flexible ones basically function as open recipients of ideas from many different sources.

The second aspect of R and D organization is *idea and project evaluation*. To begin with this type of activity may be centralized or decentralized in a company.

78

In some instances a central committee meets once or twice a year to evaluate new ideas and to decide on new projects. In other cases more decentralized evaluation takes place on lower levels of the organization, for instance product divisions may independently evaluate and decide on new ideas. Idea and project evaluation may also vary with regard to how formal the procedures are. In some companies formal, quantified critieria for selecting and following up projects are emphasized, such as precise market and cost estimates and probabilities of success (Näslund and Sellstedt, 1973). In other companies informal, intuitive appraisals carry more weight.

The third aspect of R and D organization refers to how *internal project work* is carried out. In all companies studied, project groups are used in R and D, but they may be more or less fixed or flexible. Flexible project groups may, for instance, mostly include technical researchers at early stages, while marketing experts are more numerous and influential at later stages. In addition to membership variation, flexible project groups often have different project leaders at different stages or product development. Fixed project groups, on the other hand, do not show consistent changes in group membership and leadership in response to different research requirements.

In our study an overall classification of the organization of R and D in the different companies is carried out, by employing the above distinctions. A wide and flexible external information and contact network, decentralized idea and project evaluation and flexible project groups are used as indications of a responsive organization of R and D. All these factors should tend to make it easier for a company to respond to changes in its internal and external environment by developing new products. Narrow and inflexible information networks, centralized idea and project evaluation and fixed project groups, on the other hand, should make it more difficult to respond and are therefore used as indications of a fixed organization of R and D.

The variation between companies to a large extent appears to be related to concentrated versus diversified R and D policy (Tables 6.1 and 6.5). Of the four companies classified as having a highly or relatively responsive organization of R and D all also have expressed a diversified R and D policy. Of the seven companies classified as having a highly or relatively fixed organization of R and D five have expressed a concentrated R and D policy. This apparent connection between policy and organization is functional in the sense that diversification implies more radical change in R and D conditions facing a company than concentration, and this makes a responsive organization a more logical choice than a fixed organization.

There is no clear indication from the data that company size is related to type of organization. With the exception of the chemical industry, the largest company in each industry tends, however, to have a fixed organization of R and D. There are, on the other hand, several relatively small companies in the electronic industry which have a fixed organization, and in the chemical industry the largest company has a highly responsive organization.

6.5 Open and closed R and D strategies

In Table 6.6 an attempt is made to classify overall realized R and D strategies with regard to how open or closed they are. Open strategies are more searching, flexible and adaptive to changing conditions in the internal or external technical and marketing environment of a company. It therefore follows from the previous chapters that they are more appropriate to innovative companies, who want to take advantage of the opportunities for profit and growth which are provided by a rapidly changing environment. Closed strategies, on the other hand, are more suitable for positional companies, which are mainly trying to maintain and strengthen an established position, for instance by developing new products in line with their existing technological and marketing areas of specialization.

External orientation, synergistic technology use and responsive organization of R and D may thus all be used as indications of open R and D strategies. Similarly, internal orientation, isolated technology use and fixed organization of R and D may be used as indications of closed R and D strategies.

Table 6.6. Realized R and D Strategies in Different Companies

Company	Orientation	Technology use	Organization of R and D	Overall strategy classification
P.1	Highly external (1)	Isolated/synergistic (0.5)	Highly responsive (1)	Very open (2.5
P.2	Relatively internal (0.25)	Isolated (0)	Relatively fixed (0.25)	Very closed (0.5)
P.3	Relatively external (0.75)	Isolated/synergistic (0.5)	Relatively responsive (0.75)	Relatively open (2)
S.1	Highly internal (0)	Isolated (0)	Highly fixed (0)	Very closed (0)
S.2	Highly internal (0)	Isolated (0)	Relatively fixed (0.25)	Very closed (0.25)
E.1	Highly internal (0)	Synergistic (1)	Relatively fixed (0.25)	Relatively closed (1.25)
E.2	Relatively internal (0.25)	Isolated/synergistic (0.5)	Relatively fixed (0.25)	Relatively closed (1)
E.3	Relatively internal (0.25)	Synergistic (1)	Relatively fixed (0.25)	Relatively open (1.5)
E.4	Highly external (1)	Isolated (0)	Highly fixed (0)	Relatively closed (1)
C.1	Relatively external (0.75)	Isolated/synergistic (0.5)	Highly responsive (1)	Very open (2.25)
C.2	Relatively internal (0.25)	Isolated/synergistic (0.5)	Relatively responsive (0.75)	Relatively open (1.5)

Higher numbers indicate a more open strategy.

By employing these empirical indicators we find that the pharmaceutical and chemical companies appear to have the most open strategies, while the electronic and, in particular, the steel companies have the most closed strategies. But at the same time we see that variation between companies within industries is substantial, with for instance one of the pharmaceutical companies having a very closed strategy and one of the chemical companies having a much more open strategy than the other one.

If we compare with R and D policy (Table 6.1) we seen that innovative companies tend to have more open strategies and positional companies more closed. If we rank the companies from most innovative to most positional policy and from most open to most closed strategy, the Spearman rank correlation coefficient is 0.48, indicating a relatively strong correlation between the two sets of data (almost significant at the five per cent level). Companies, thus, tend to employ strategies which are consistent with their overall R and D policy, if we accept the line of reasoning emphasized in the distinction between innovative and positional companies. But it still remains to study the outcome of different R and D strategies to estimate how successful they have been.

Summing up this section, it appears that — as in the case of R and D policies — there are interesting differences between industries and companies with regard to realized R and D strategies. These differences probably reflect both differences in market and technological requirements, and in the relative success of different companies in carrying out R and D.

6.6 Measuring the success of R and D

In order to be able to determine the relative success of different R and D strategies — policies and activities — we need to be able to measure the outcome of R and D along relevant dimensions. Sales figures for different products — which at first thought seem appropriate measures — are at second thought highly problematic. To begin with such data for product life cycles are not readily available, and cannot be directly related to R and D strategies. Such strategies are primarily concerned with *product design,* while sales figures also reflect marketing variables, such as price, advertising and distribution. Consequently there is a need to find indications of success, which are directly related to what we want to study, differences in product design between competing products.

The main outcome measure for R and D used here is the *level of technological innovation*. This refers to the extent to which the basic product design utilizes advanced technology, previously not applied to the problem area. A product representing a high level of technological innovation therefore is a radically new product from a technological point of view. Such a product often, but by no means always, also is a unique product from a market introduction point of view, with little or no competition from other products.

Unique products, on the other hand, need not, and often do, represent a high level of technological innovation. If the level of technological innovation is low, however, and patent protection cannot be obtained, product imitation by competitors usually takes place rapidly if the product is a success on the market. The company first on the market is then only assured a short-lived competitive advantage. When the level of technological innovation is high, on the other hand, a company may expect to gain a more long run advantage, even if it cannot obtain patent protection. This is because its advanced technical knowledge and competence and qualified technical facilities usually make it difficult for competing companies to imitate the product.

The level of technological innovation, therefore, is used in this analysis as the main and most important measure of success in R and D, for products which have gained market acceptance. It may be expected to lead to a more long run competitive advantage, than merely being alone on the market with a new product at the time of its introduction. If it is possible to combine a high level of technological innovation with strong patent protection, the competitive advantage is of course strengthened. But even in the absence of such protection a high level of technological innovation usually leads to a decisive competitive advantage over competing companies.

In the first analysis of the data a composite measure of success for R and D, including immediate market position for a new product and degree of patent protection was employed. The result was that level of technological innovation most clearly distinguished between successful and less successful strategies for R and D, as may be expected from the above discussion. In the present context, therefore, the level of technological innovation will be used in discussing the outcome of R and D strategies. The more complete discussion is found in the original report (Nyström, 1977).

The level of technological innovation for each new product included in the study — as well as the other outcome measures for R and D not reported on here in detail — were assessed on the basis of interview data. The classfication scale used was from 1–5, with higher values denoting a higher level of innovation. The average level of technological innovation for all products and companies is 3.7 on this scale, with the chemical and pharmaceutical companies showing the highest values (4.2 and 3.8) and the electronic and steel companies the lowest (3.6 and 3.8). The intra-industry variation, however, is quite substantial, especially in the steel industry (2.8–3.9) and in the electronic industry (3.4–4.2) and we find the smallest variation in the chemical industry (4.0–4.3).

If we compare the level of technological innovation for new products with their market position at the time of introduction, we find that new products with a high level of technological innovation usually also have a strong market position. In the steel and electronic industries, however, the data indicates that the market position for new products often is quite strong, even when the level of technological innovation is quite low. In these cases, as we have noted above, product imitation may be expected to take place rather rapidly, and the competitive advantage of the company will then not last long. Since patent protection according to the data is particularly difficult to obtain for new products in the electronic and steel industries — even when the level of technological innovation is high — the competitive advantages of new products for companies in these industries, should tend to be even more limited, compared to the chemical and pharmaceutical industries, where patent protection evidently is much easier to achieve.

Both the average level of technological innovation, and the chances of obtaining strong patent protection at any given level of innovation, thus appear to be higher in the chemical and pharmaceutical industries, compared to the electronic and steel industries. To some extent this relative advantage is offset, however, by the very favourable market position which companies, according to the data, are often able to achieve, for new products in the electronic and steel industry. Market protection, for instance achieved by tying customers closely to a company, may then be a substitute for technological or patent protection, as we have seen in the discussion of company policies for R and D, companies appear to be aware of this.

For our purpose, however, the differences in R and D outcome between industries and companies are mainly of interest to the extent that they reflect differences in company R and D policies and realized strategies, rather than in general environmental conditions facing industries. To try to analyse such company relationships one starting point is to look at differences between products regardless of company. Since so many different and complex factors are intertwined on the company level, direct conclusions on this level on how action affects outcome are difficult to draw. By first studying if general product characteristics appear to be related to success in the overall data, a firmer basis for drawing conclusions on the company level should be possible. Such product characteristics emphasized in our study are idea generation and technology use.

For all products combined, *external orientation is associated in our data with a higher level of technological innovation, than internal orientation* (4.0 versus 3.4). To simplify the analysis without changing the main tendencies involved, orientation is measured by idea generation alone, rather than both idea generation and product development. As we have seen in Table 6.2, these two sets of data display essentially the same picture.

If we look at industries we find basically the same results, the only exception being the steel industry. Here only three of 23 products are the result of external ideas, and these on the average show a much lower level of technological innovation than internal ideas (3.4 versus 4.0). In all other industries external ideas are associated with a higher level of technological innovation than internal ideas (Table 6.7). A larger number of products, however, are the result of internal ideas (54 of 91). The main exception to this is found in the pharmaceutical industry, where 15 out of 24 products are classified as based on external idea generation, while the chemical industry shows a slight overweight for external ideas (seven of 13).

In summary, external ideas in most industries are associated with more successful products than internal ideas, but only in the pharmaceutical industry is there a clear tendency for external ideas also to lead to a larger number of new products. In the steel and electronic industries, internal ideas have led to many

Table 6.7. Level of Technological Innovation for Products in Relation to Technology Use and Orientation

	Level of technological innovation				
	All companies	Pharm companies	Steel companies	Electronic companies	Chemical companies
Synergistic use of technology	4, 0 (33)	4, 3 (8)	4, 0 (3)	3, 6 (18)	4, 5 (6)
Isolated use of technology	3, 5 (58)	3, 5 (16)	3, 4 (20)	3, 5 (15)	3, 9 (7)
External idea	4, 0 (37)	4, 0 (15)	3, 0 (3)	4, 0 (12)	4, 3 (7)
Internal idea	3, 4 (54)	3, 3 (9)	3, 6 (20)	3, 2 (19)	4, 0 (6)

Higher values indicate higher average level of technological innovation for products concerned. Number of products for each category in parentheses.

more new products than external ideas, but while these products have been quite successful in the steel industry, they have been less successful than products based on external ideas in the electronic industry. In the chemical industry the difference between external and internal ideas is not so pronounced, either with regard to number of new products or level of technological innovation.

If we turn our attention to the technology component of realized strategy, *synergistic use of technology is associated with a higher level of technological innovation* for all products combined (4.0 versus 3.5). This relationship is found in all industries, but is most pronounced in the pharmaceutical industry and least pronounced in the electronic industry (Table 6.7). In the overall data a majority of new products are the result of isolated technology use (58 of 91). This holds true in all industries, except the electronic industry.

As in the case of external ideas, but even more consistently for all industries, synergistic technology use thus is associated with technically more advanced new products. Isolated technology use, however, similar to internal ideas, has led to more new products. This points to the conclusion that it is more difficult to find new products by combining technologies, but when found they tend to be more successful.

If we extend the product analysis to apply to companies (Table 6.8), some comments may be made which, while highly tentative, suggest that companies should consider the types of organizational and technological determinants of success in R and D, proposed in this chapter.

To begin with we may expect companies whose realized strategies are consistent with their expressed policies to be more successful in R and D than

84

Table 6.8. R and D Policy, Realized Strategy and Technological Outcome
for the Different Companies

Company	R and D policy	Realized R and D strategy	Level of technological innovation
P.1	Highly innovative	Very open	3.9
P.2	Highly innovative	Very closed	3.4
P.3	Highly innovative	Relatively open	4.2
S.1	Relatively innovative	Very closed	3.9
S.2	Highly positional	Very closed	2.8
E.1	Relatively positional	Relatively closed	3.5
E.2	Relatively positional	Relatively closed	3.7
E.3	Relatively positional	Relatively open	3.0
E.4	Relatively innovative	Relatively closed	4.0
C.1	Highly innovative	Very open	4.3
C.2	Relatively innovative	Relatively open	4.0

companies whose strategies are inconsistent. A consistent combination of policy and realized strategy, as we have pointed out before, means that a more innovative policy should be accompanied by a more open realized strategy and a more positional policy by a more closed strategy. We have seen that there is a relatively strong tendency in our data for innovative policies to be accompanied by open strategies and positional policies by closed strategies. But companies, to be successful, must also choose policies which are appropriate for the external and internal marketing and technological environments in which they will be operating. Furthermore, they must employ realized strategies which are internally consistent, that is, with components which work together to provide the desired results.

Market and technological conditions, by definition, may be expected to vary more between than within industries. Comparability between companies with regard to external environmental conditions will be sought, therefore, by restricting the direct analysis of the outcome of company R and D strategies to intra-industry comparisons (Table 6.8).

If we begin with the pharmaceutical industry, all three companies express a highly innovative policy, stressing diversification through technically based, offensive R and D. The first and the third company, however, appear to have employed a more open realized strategy, than the second company. They show a more external orientation, synergistic use of technology and responsive organization of R and D. They also have been considerably more successful in the technological outcome of their R and D (3.9 and 4.2 versus 3.4). These results, then, support our basic tenet that innovative companies working in highly dynamic technical and marketing environments — such as those facing the pharmaceutical companies in our study — should employ open realized strategies for R and D. If we turn to the steel industry, the differences between the two companies are substantial, both with regard to policy and realized strategy. The first steel company has a more innovative policy than the second company, but both companies emphasize concentration rather than diversification. The former company balances this positional tendency by an offensive technical orientation, thereby displaying greater innovative concern in its policy, than the latter company, which has a more defensive, market orientation. Both companies employ a very closed realized strategy, emphasizing internal orientation, isolated technology use and a fixed organization of R and D.

The differences in success for R and D between the two steel companies are very pronounced, with the first steel company showing a much higher level of technological innovation (3.9 versus 2.8). The more successful steel company has been able to achieve its higher level of technological innovation by using a very closed strategy. It has relied almost entirely on its own internal competence and on an isolated use of technology. The less successful steel company has tried to pursue a similar, but less extreme strategy.

At first thought, and when we compare with the pharmaceutical companies, it might seem that the first steel company would have been even more successful if it had implemented its relatively innovative policy by a more open realized strategy. This may be the case, but we must remember the special environmental conditions facing the steel companies. In this industry diversification into new product areas — the perhaps main concern of an innovative policy — is highly restricted by the inflexibility of production and marketing. In other words, diversification — which the successful steel company does not seek — might be facilitated by a more open strategy, but it is not likely that such an open strategy, as in the case of the innovative pharmaceutical companies would lead to many radically new products, in line with the production and marketing requirements of the company.

The main differences, instead, between the two steel companies, according to our data, is that the more successful company has an offensive and technically based R and D policy, and the internal resources and competence to implement this policy well, by using a highly closed realized strategy. The less successful company has a defensive and market based policy less suitable for achieving success in the industry, and has also not been successful in implementing its somewhat more open realized strategy. In this case the more open strategy is probably the result of the company feeling that its internal competence, in its established technology areas, is not quite what it should be, rather than representing an effort to diversify into new areas of technology.

Being technically ahead of competitors in a company's established area of technology apparently is a major success factor in the steel industry, and the first steel company has been highly successful in this respect. This basically requires a positional policy, and the classification of the first company as relatively innovative is somewhat misleading in this case, since one of the basic requirements for an innovative policy, diversification, is lacking. This points to the need for using more complex and differentiated measures of policy in future studies, which is not surprising since the present study represents a first attempt to develop and measure the introduced concepts.

In the electronic industry the four companies show quite similar overall policies and realized strategies for R and D, emphasizing relatively positional policies and closed realized strategies. If we look more closely at the policy and strategy components, however, the differences become more striking. The first electronic company, for instance, has a diversified and defensive policy, while the other electronic companies have concentrated and offensive policies.

The first two electronic companies appear to be quite successful in choosing and combining policy and realized strategy. The first company's relatively closed strategy, emphasizing synergistic technology use and internal orientation, seems well suited for carrying out its relatively positional, defensive and market based policy. The second company's more offensive and concentrated policy, also seems to have been carried out quite well, by its relatively closed, internally oriented strategy with somewhat isolated use of technology. Both companies show quite high values for the average outcome of their R and D (3.5 and 3.7).

The third electronic company appears to have been somewhat less successful in choosing and implementing its policy. Its relatively open strategy, with synergistic use of technology and external orientation, seems to have been unduly constrained by its relatively positional, concentrated and market based policy. This seems to have led to a fairly low value for the outcome of its R and D (3.0). The fourth electronic company is a very young company, the policy and realized strategy of which had not yet been sufficiently stabilized to permit conclusions with regard to how appropriate they were for its activities.

In the chemical industry the first chemical company expresses a highly innovative policy and the second chemical company a relatively innovative one. In both companies diversification is combined with offensiveness, but while the first company has a quite technically based policy, the second company has a more market based one. Consistent with their policies, the first company has a highly open and the second company a fairly open realized strategy. The difference is that the first company shows a more external orientation and greater synergistic use of technology.

Both chemical companies are quite successful in their R and D, with a somewhat higher value for the first company (4.3 versus 4.0). We thus find, as in the case of the pharmaceutical companies, that a more external orientation and greater synergistic use of technology is associated with a higher level of technological innovation. The first, more successful chemical company has a relatively external orientation and highly responsive organization of R and D, while the second has a relatively internal orientation and a somewhat less responsive organization of R and D. In our study the first pharmaceutical company and the first pharmaceutical company are the two companies who most widely and actively have searched outside the company for ideas for new products. They are also two of the most successful companies with regard to the technological outcome of their R and D.

6.7 Summary of Chapter 6

The empirical study reported on this chapter illustrates the possibility and usefulness of applying the general approach to company development put forward in this book, to a specific area of investigation, company strategies for R and D. The results indicate that important differences exist between companies of the types assumed in our theoretical discussion, and that these differences are related to differences in company development and performance.

To begin with both external orientation and synergistic technology use appear to be consistently related to the success of R and D strategies, by leading to a higher level of technological innovation for new products. In a general sense both these innovative elements of company strategy — broadening and combining elements of thought — were emphasized in Chapter 4, as implying favourable conditions for company creativity. These results, thus, give support to the general conclusion in this book that companies need to have an open and flexible approach to strategic decision making under changing conditions. They also show that companies need organizational flexibility and diversity to stimulate company creativity as argued in Chapters 3 and 4.

We also find in our data clear differences between companies with regard to positional and innovative elements in R and D policy and realized strategy. Diversification, technological orientation and offensiveness are then taken as indications of innovative policy and concentration, market orientation and defensiveness as indications of positional policy. External orientation, synergistic technology use and responsive organization of R and D are used to indicate an open realized R and D strategy and internal orientation, isolated use of technology and fixed organization of R and D to indicate a closed strategy.

Following our previous discussion we should then expect positional companies to prefer closed realized strategies and innovative companies open realized strategies, as appropriate to carrying out their expressed policies. In our data we find a relatively strong tendency for innovative policies to be accompanied by open realized strategies, and positional policies to be accompanied by closed realized strategies, which gives support to such a situational view of strategic decision making.

The main purpose of the chapter, however, has not been to test specific propositions. It rather has been to explore the possibilities of using the approach to gain a better overall understanding of company development, by focusing on a highly crucial area of strategic decision making company strategies for R and D — which so far has received little attention. In this sense it reflects more the overall concern of this book, than the specific problems dealt with.

CHAPTER 7

A Cognitive Psychological Approach to Strategy Formulation

7.1 Introduction

At the beginning of this book the need to consider both continuous and discontinuous change in an innovative theory of the firm was stated as a basic requirement. Examples of discontinuous change are new products, new production techniques and new organization forms. These represent innovations and, if they are successful, company creativity. Continuous changes, on the other hand, are gradual adjustments, such as product modifications or technical adjustments.

To be able to theoretically explain and empirically understand discontinuous change — as a strategic element in company development — we need to consider psychological factors relating to individual decision making. This is a basic assumption of the present approach, which sets it apart from most other treatments of company development.

The discussion of company creativity in Chapter 4 underlines the importance of psychological differences between individuals in how they organize and develop their world views as a basis for developing company strategies. But company structure is also of importance for company development, as we have noted in Chapter 2. The present chapter, therefore, attempts to bring together strategy formulation and company structure in analysing the process of company development.

Our integrated analysis of the process of company development is based on the distinction between positional, innovative and latent positional/innovative companies, presented in Chapter 2. Since this classification scheme allows for transitions from one type of company to another — as a result of factors internal or external to the company — it is well suited for a dynamic analysis of company development.

To explain specific instances of company development within the structural constraints implied by a company's innovative potential, we need, however, to study in more detail than we have so far, the overall strategic component, which we have called innovative orientation.

In this chapter, therefore, a cognitive classification model will first be presented (Nyström, 1974), which considers the influence of both subjective uncertainty and objective information on individual decision making, as a crucial component affecting innovative orientation in companies.

By employing this model we may theoretically discuss both continuous change and discontinuous development. The approach is an attempt to explain strategy formulation on the company level by individual cognitive processes. Thereby we may better understand why different companies under similar environmental conditions often chose quite different development strategies.

In addition, our integrated psychological and organizational makes it possible, as well, to introduce and explain changes over time in company orientation, for instance from innovative to positional. This, then, may be viewed as due to the interaction between structure and strategy. The former is determined by factors such as economic resources and organizational relationships, and the latter by the cognitive processes of leading decision makers.

Cyclical variation over time in sales and profits, perhaps accompanied by changes in organization and marketing strategy, will usually characterize actual company development. This type of variation is often not possible to directly account for by changes outside the company, for instance in economic climate or market conditions.

By emphasizing both internal company factors and outside change in a cognitive, psychological approach to strategy formulation we hopefully will be able to better understand company development in these instances. An attempt will be made in the following to test this proposition by applying the proposed type of analysis to an empirical example, which summarizes the common development features of a number of Swedish Development Companies during the 1960s.

7.2 A cognitive model of decision making

In this section a cognitive model of organizational decision making will be presented. Unlike other cognitive approaches to organizational decision making (March and Simon, 1958; Cyert and March, 1963), which emphasize general cognitive mechanisms and limitations, the suggested approach considers *differences* in cognitive functioning between individuals. It may therefore be seen as suggesting a 'psychological contingency approach' to organizational decision making and in this sense is in line with recent general developments in the literature towards more conditional organizational analysis. As in other cognitive approaches to organizational decision making, the assumption is made that organizational action basically depends on individual decisions. Group interaction, as in the case of company creativity, is assumed to modify, but not radically change, the nature of the individual decision processes.

Our cognitive model differs from the type of statistical approach to decision making, normally employed in economic and business-administrative models, of company behaviour (Lamberton, 1971; Carlson, 1973). These models implicitly assume that uncertainty may be eliminated by collecting and statistically analysing data. In relatively stable and simple development situations, characterized by gradual, continuous change, this is both feasible and desirable from a company planning point of view. In development situations characterized by highly complex and changing, non-repetitious factors, we need, however, a different view of uncertainty reduction to understand actual company decision making.

Genuine uncertainty (Shackle 1958), that is uncertainty which cannot be reduced by statistical techniques, then dominates the picture. To understand how decisions are made in the face of such uncertainty, we need a cognitive, rather than statistical approach to decision making. Such a view focuses on how decision makers react to perceived uncertainty by restructuring their cognitive models of the relevant universe, rather than on the statistical means for removing uncertainty.

Our cognitive model is mainly designed to make possible a better understanding of decision making, when genuine uncertainty is a major concern. To the extent that uncertainty may be eliminated by statistical means, but decision makers are unable or unwilling to do so — perhaps to save the cost of collecting and analysing data — the model will, however, be applicable also to more predictable situations.

In contrast to the predominantly normative orientation of statistical appraches to decision making, the proposed psychological approach is more descriptive, and in this sense the two approaches are complementary, rather than competing. At the same time, however, the distinction between normative and descriptive becomes increasingly difficult to maintain in the face of genuine uncertainty. In situations highly characterized by such uncertainty, it is not possible with any great degree of accuracy to tell decision makers what to do on the basis of what will happen, and what they do then takes on added interest.

The role of *information* is a crucial point of difference between a more normative statistical approach to decision making in situations characterized by risk — where probabilities may be assigned — and the proposed cognitive approach for situations characterized by genuine uncertainty, where such probabilities cannot be estimated. In statistical approaches increases in information — that is in awareness of relevant empirical factors — are usually assumed to reduce uncertainly both in estimates of probabilities and in the decision maker's subjective belief in these estimates. In our proposed cognitive approach, however, added information may — depending on the circumstances — either *decrease* or *increase* the subjective uncertainty of the decision maker, which in this case is not tied to estimates of probabilities, but to his general view of the problem area.

In order to appreciate the differences between the suggested cognitive approach and more statistically oriented approaches to decision making in economic theory and in economic models of organizations, we may compare *lack of information* with *incorrect information* (Boulding, 1966). This distinction is not made in economic theory, since all information is then assumed to be correct. From the point of view of a cognitive approach an assumption of perfect information would imply that all cognitive structures are accurate — but perhaps not complete — representations of relevant external factors. Obviously this is not a very realistic assumption in most instances of organizational decision making in complex and changing environments.

If we assume that we can tell in advance whether information is correct or not, it is natural to apply a statistical approach to decision making and collect and process further information up to the point where the incremental cost is greater than the incremental gain in information. In situations characterized by genuine uncertainty, however, such assessments are not possible. In order to study how, in spite of this limitation, decision makers achieve determinate decisions we need a different approach, which recognizes cognitive mechanisms for structuring information.

Uncertainty gap, differentiation and causal linking

Our suggested approach to decision making, in contrast to statistical decision models, focuses on the *structure* (Rokeach, 1960) rather than the *content* of the decision basis of an individual. Subjective uncertainty is defined not as lack of information — that is as incomplete information which may be made complete by collecting and processing further information — but as *lack of cognitive structure*, in situations when there is an uncertainty gap between the structure and the decision makers belief in this structure. Cognitive structure is necessary to achieve determinate decisions in the face of a multitude of opportunities but need not — and in situations involving genuine uncertainty cannot — be associated with a high degree of statistical predictability. Instead of analysing how such predictability may be achieved, our cognitive approach thus centers on a decision maker's cognitive structure of a problem area, and on how information available to the decision maker may influence this structure (Gardner and Schoen, 1962; Scott, 1963; Bieri and coworkers, 1966; Schroder, Driver and Streufert, 1967).

A cognitive structure may be defined as a set of partially ordered cognitive elements — notions or ideas — which are viewed by the decision maker as relevant for determining the outcome of a contemplated decision. The relations between the elements may be either implicit — that is intuitive — or viewed as being in an explicit cause and effect relationship to each other.

There are two dimensions of cognitive structures that would appear to be of particular interest in this connection. One is the degree of detail which a certain structure contains, or in other words how *differentiated* it is. The other is the extent to which a certain structure is causally linked, i.e. how interrelated different elements are. These aspects will be examined in relation to whether or not an *uncertainty gap* is experienced by the decision maker, with regard to a specific cognitive structure. The less his belief in the cognitive structure as an adequate representation of relevant factors, the greater the uncertainty gap.

Two cases will now be distinguished between in our discussion. In the first case no initial uncertainty gap exists, i.e. the decision maker is assumed not to experience any general uncertainty with regard to the outcome of a contemplated decision, He, then, may be assumed to have little motivation to actively seek additional information. In the event that he is a passive recipient of information pertaining to the relevant decision this information will, from his subjective point of view, be more or less disturbing. If it does not conform to his prior point of view it is highly likely that in many instances he will assimilate this information into his existing cognitive structure and then his subjective uncertainty will not be affected (Festinger, 1957).

Neither the degree of differentiation nor the causal linking will be influenced in this instance, and from a decision making point of view the information will have been neutral. It is of course possible that the information will instead be viewed as conflicting with the initial views of the decision maker, especially if it indicates a previously unnoticed, serious threat to the future of the organization. In this latter instance the increase in information leads to a greater subjective uncertainty, instead of to less, as statistical approaches usually assume. If an uncertainty gap develops our second case will become applicable.

In this second case, the decision maker thus is assumed to experience general uncertainty with regard to the outcome of a contemplated decision, which means that an uncertainty gap exists between his cognitive structure and his belief in this structure.

This is the case we are primarily interested in, since it is most likely to reflect organizational decision making in genuinely uncertain situations, characterized by unique events. When an uncertainty gap exists active information collecting and processing aimed at achieving a subjectively more satisfactory cognitive structure of relevant factors, will be assumed to take place. The more undifferentiated and devoid of causal links a cognitive structure is, the stronger the tendency is assumed to be for the individual to seek information, which may reduce the uncertainty gap. Both differentiation and the establishment of causal links are in principle viewed as cognitive mechanisms which may reduce or eliminate the uncertainty gap associated with a particular decision.

A cognitive model of strategy formulation

As a basis for our continued discussion a cognitive development model will now be presented. By employing this model we may consider both continuous and discontinuous changes in company orientation, based on individual assessments of environmental opportunities and uncertainties. Perceived uncertainty, then, is assumed to create a tendency for information gathering and processing, as a basis for cognitive restructuring on the individual level and strategic reorientation on the company level. In our model this is represented by the existence of an uncertainty gap, and the cognitive mechanisms for reducing subjective uncertainty (differentiation and/or causal linking).

By classifying the degree of causal linking in the cognitive structure of a decision maker relevant to a certain decision problem as either high or low, and the degree of differentiation of the structure also as high or low, we can construct

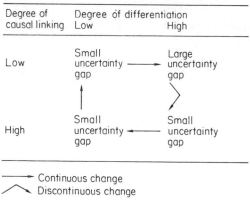

Figure 7.1. A Cognitive Model of Strategy Formulation

a two-by-two classification table of cognitive structure (Figure 7.1). By utilizing this table we can discuss and try to provide a plausible explanation of cognitive development on the level of the individual decision maker, as a basis for understanding company development strategies.

To begin with we will assume that the cognitive structure of the decision maker is vague and intuitive, i.e. characterized by both a low degree of differentiation and a low degree of causal linking. If the decision maker is satisfied with the performance of the organization with regard to the type of action implied by the structure, he may well not experience any uncertainty gap. He will then, according to our assumptions not actively seek information pertaining to the decision area and if he passively receives such information he will tend to assimilate it into his structure, without changing it. This decision situation corresponds to the upper left hand side in Figure 7.1.

If, however, for some reason the decision maker becomes uncertain with regard to his overall conception and evaluation of the problem — for instance as a result of company performance falling below expectations — he will, according to our assumptions, actively seek information to gain a better understanding of relevant events. He may, for instance, seek more detailed information through market research or better coordination of information within the organization by improving its central information system. In this way both the degree of differentiation and, subsequently, the degree of causal linking should tend to increase. The decision situation, then, changes from the upper left hand to the upper right hand, and then to the lower right hand side in Figure 7.1.

The development from low to high degree of differentiation may be seen as a continuous process of gaining a better, but not fundamentally different, cognitive structure of a decision problem. In other words, the degree of causal linking need not initially undergo radical change, indeed it probably will not, since understanding presupposes knowledge. It generally takes some time to assimilate new information, before new implications may be drawn, and therefore an incubation period is likely, as we have noted in our discussion of creativity in Chapter 4.

An increase in differentiation does not, therefore, guarantee a higher degree of causal linking and new insight. Instead it may merely lead to greater confusion, if the conditions for creativity are absent. A continuous process of gaining better knowledge, without upsetting previously established relationships, is typical for statistical approaches to decision making.

If however, the conditions are favourable for a restructuring of the problem, it is likely that after some time a discontinuous change will take place in the cognitive structure. After a certain threshold has been reached in increased differentiation — without a reorganization of the causal linking between cognitive elements — the structure may no longer be able to accommodate continuous change, and instead a new structure will become necessary.

Up until now the degree of causal linking may have changed to some extent, but preexisting links have probably precluded large changes without breaking up the existing pattern. After the restructuring a higher degree of causal linking may well be achieved, but the main point is that a *different* pattern of causal relationships will be established. This pattern will probably also have different development implications for the organization than the old one.

In contrast to the continuous process of improving the decision basis, evident in the transition from the upper left to the upper right hand side in Figure 7.1, the discontinuous process which the transition from the upper right to the lower right illustrates, cannot be analysed in terms of a statistical approach to decision making, based on an incremental process of successive refinement of the decision basis. Instead a cognitive approach is necessary to allow for both continuous and discontinuous change, which means both refining and restructuring the problem.

If we apply a systems terminology the problem can be stated as requiring both continuous functions and discontinuous step functions (Ashby, 1960), where in the latter case changes in functional relationships take place, after certain threshold values have been reached.

When we have reached the lower, right hand side in our cognitive classification scheme, it is likely that the continuous process of refining the cognitive structure — interrupted by the discontinuous change leading to reorientation — will continue within the restraints of the new structure.

The more this process leads to a more highly differentiated and causally linked structure, the smaller the uncertainty gap will probably become. Since we have assumed that the tendency to actively seek information depends on the uncertainty gap, this process of refining the cognitive structure will be self-regulating; the smaller the uncertainty gap, the less the tendency to actively seek new information.

In order to provide a plausible explanation of why this process of successive refinement may be reversed within a given structure, we must make an additional assumption with regard to cognitive structures. This assumption — which is consistent with what is generally known about cognitive processes — is that there is a built-in tendency towards *simple cognitive structures* (Miller, 1967).

In other words, high degrees of differentiation and causal linking are not by themselves desirable, from an internal functional point of view. They are rather forced by external conditions, in our analysis working via the uncertainty gap. When external conditions are viewed as stable and favourable the uncertainty gap is closed. This, then, leads not only to a slowing down and ending of the process of refining the cognitive structure, but also to a tendency to simplify it.

The process of differentiation then is reversed and a continuous process towards simplification is started. This is an internal process which may be assumed to continue as long as conflicting external information does not again lead to the development of an uncertainty gap.

In Figure 7.1 this means a continuous development in cognitive structure from the lower right to the lower left, which involves a decrease in the degree of differentiation. Since this simplification will probably begin with the elimination of cognitive elements which are relatively isolated from other elements, the degree of causal linking, to begin with, will probably not decrease substantially. Over time, however, it is conceivable that the simplification process will also tend to lead to a decrease in the degree of cognitive linking, as long as no uncertainty gap exists.

Thus Figure 7.1 may be seen as illustrating our proposed dynamic model of cognitive development. In this model uncertainty and information interact and together tend to lead to continuous and discontinuous changes in cognitive structures. In our analysis of company development these structures are the basis for making strategic decisions, and thus central to understanding company innovation.

Differences in cognitive style

By employing the proposed cognitive model, differences in cognitive style between different organizational decision makers may be considered systematically. Differences of this type are usually not taken into account in organizational analyses, probably more due to lack of adequate models, than to lack of empirical interest. Instead, as we have noted before, both economic theory and most models in organization theory assume that all decision makers have the same information available and react to it in the same way.

By employing our cognitive model we may consider differences in how individuals react to and use information to build up their world views. We may, for instance, distinguish between different modes of decision making and fundamentally different ways of using data to reach decisions. That such differences exist and are of great importance for understanding strategic decision making has been pointed out (Mintzberg, 1973b; Mintzberg and coworkers, 1976; McKenney and Keen, 1974), but few attempts have been made to systematically analyse this problem.

One such distinction with a long history in the philosophical and psychological literature is intuitive versus analytical thinking (Peters and Hammond, 1974). By pulling together the threads of our discussion of creativity in Chapter 4 and of cognitive processes in the present chapter, this distinction may be usefully incorporated into our discussion.

Intuitive thinking is directed towards overall appraisal, while analytical thinking focuses on specific relationships. In the former case the relationships between a large number of cognitive elements are implied, rather than explicit. This ties intuition more to differentiation than to causal linking. In other words, the number and variety of aspects considered then is more crucial to the decision arrived at, than specific cause–effect relationships. Analytical decision making, on the other hand, is directed towards establishing and using explicit relationships, that is causal linking is the main issue.

According to our previous discussion of the conditions for creativity, intuitive thinking and decision making should therefore be of great importance during the early, exploratory phases of the creative process. During the later, delimiting and verifying stages, analytical thought processes seem more appropriate.

Furthermore, individuals evidently differ in their inclination and ability for intuitive versus analytical thinking and problem solving (McKenney and Keen, 1974). It should therefore be possible to utilize the type of approach suggested here to achieve better conformity between organizational problems and the capacity of individuals to handle them. Highly uncertain decision problems require more intuitively oriented individuals and a wide information base, while more predictable problems are better suited for analytically oriented individuals and specific information.

Individual differences in cognitive style may also help to explain differences in organizational style. From an economic point of view puzzling differences between companies with regard to innovation may, for instance, become better understandable, if we allow for individual differences in cognitive style among decision makers.

Against the background of our company classification model, we may hypothesize the positional companies, in their appropriate environments, would benefit by a large proportion of analytically oriented decision makers. In these companies, defining and delimiting existing problems is of primary importance, which requires much analytical effort. In innovative companies, on the other hand, the need for intuitive decision making should be greater, due to the greater need for finding and exploring new areas of investigation.

7.3 An integrated psychological and organizational analysis of company development

An attempt will now be made, in an empirical context, to extend and more fully develop our company classification model — distinguishing between positional and innovative companies — by employing our cognitive model of decision making.

Since these models refer to different levels of analysis — company versus individual — there is a problem in combining the two. As in the rest of the book this will be achieved by assuming that organizational decisions basically reflect and may be studied through individual decisions, with group processes modifying, but not radically changing the results. This, of course, is a consensus view of organizational decision making, centering on the need for and possibility of common action, rather than on conflicts between opposing views.

To show the full range of development possibilities it is suitable to begin with an organization in its early stages of development. In order, however, to find a manageable time period to study, a special type of company, the Investment Development Company, has been chosen for our discussion. Characteristic for this type of company is that it is a combination of previously existing companies, rather than a completely new company. This joining together of previously independent enterprises may from an organizational point of view be viewed as the starting of a new organization. At the same time, however, the development process is speeded up by the fact that the components of the new organization are from a technical and marketing point of view already established. This makes it easier to collect data on the type of changes we are interested in, and to isolate these changes from other changes in company environment.

The following discussion does not refer to one specific company. Instead it is based on the common development characteristics of a number of Investment Development Companies in Sweden, which in retrospect appear to have experienced similar problems and attacted these problems in similar ways. The data was collected by another researcher, who in collaboration with me found the framework presented here useful for understanding and analysing the development situation of these companies. For a fuller presentation of the empirical data the reader is referred to his report (Jönsson, 1973).

By their very nature, Investment Development Companies are usually, at least to begin with, highly decentralized companies without consistent overall patterns of behaviour. In Sweden companies of this type were formed during the 1960s to provide better expansion possibilities for a number of small and medium sized enterprises, through better financing and improved technical and organizational planning.

Initially, however, these Investment Development Companies in Sweden met with great coordination problems between subunits, which often were organized quite differently from one and another and operated under various market conditions. As long as general business conditions were favourable the individual enterprises could, however, continue to operate as they had before, and central management did not find it necessary to interfere. This, however, meant that the anticipated benefits of joining together the companies were not being realized.

From the point of view of our company classification model, the Investment Development Companies, to begin with, could thus be seen as being relatively positional. No clear innovative orientation — willingness to change the existing activities to better utilize the total potentials of the companies — apparently existed, and the lack of coordination within the Development Companies evidently made any consistent overall company stategies difficult to carry out. In other words, both innovative potential and innovative orientation evidently were largely lacking in the early development of these companies.

It is interesting to compare this company classification with the implications of our cognitive decision model. In the early stages of company development it seems from the interview data that the cognitive structures of central management in the Investment Development Companies with regard to overall company behaviour were not very well developed. No central information systems existed to coordinate information from different subunits and each part of a company usually had its own accounting and planning system. This must have made it difficult for companies to achieve overall assessments of their development possibilities. From the data their cognitive structures regarding strategic development thus appear to have been relatively undifferentiated and fragmented, that is with a low degree of causal linking.

At the same time most decision makers evidently did not experience large uncertainty gaps, with regard to how good representations of reality their structures were. Company performance was satisfactory in most instances, which according to our previous discussion gave little cause for concern, with regard to how valid and adequate prevailing ideas and notions about company development were. In other words, top managers appear to have had rather vague and unsystematic ideas about total company development, and were not strongly motivated to question these views, as long as company performance was satisfactory. Their passive approach to company development and lack of innovative orientation is consistent with this interpretation of their behaviour.

At the end of the 1960s the economic situation of the Investment Development Companies underwent radical change. Profits suddenly dropped, partly due to changes in overall economic conditions. This crisis led to widespread reorganization in these companies, stressing central control and coordination of subunits. Accounting and planning procedures were for instance standardized within companies, and central auditing and control systems were introduced.

Against the background of our cognitive model we may assume that these negative changes in economic performance led to uncertainty gaps in the minds of top managers, with regard to their conceptions of development possibilities. According to our model, this should then have created tendencies towards higher degrees of differentiation and, subsequently, higher degrees of cognitive linking, in their cognitive structures relating to company developments. It should also have made them more willing to consider change in overall company strategy and to develop a clear innovative orientation.

In our cognitive classification model this means a transition first from the top left hand side to the top right hand side, and then to the bottom right hand side (Figure 7.1). In our company classification model the development of a clear innovative orientation implies a transition from a positional company to a latent positional/innovative company (Figure 2.1).

According to our discussion in Chapter 2 this, however, implies an inherently unstable development situation, since strategy and structure are not in balance in latent positional/innovative companies. Even if external conditions remain the same, we may therefore expect that the company will tend to change, either back to a positional company or into an innovative company.

In the empirical situation we are discussing the development of clear innovative orientation apparently also led to other organizational changes in the companies concerned. They, for instance, introduced greater flexibility into their organization structures, primarily by improving intraorganizational communication and interaction. In this case, therefore, the companies developed into innovative companies according to our company classification model, by developing innovative potential, in addition to innovative orientation.

In Chapter 2 we concluded that innovative companies, as well as positional companies, may be expected to be inherently more stable than latent positional/innovative companies. By using our cognitive model we may now, however, further qualify that statement. By noting that the clear innovative orientation in innovative companies may be expected to tend to disappear, if a company is successful over a long period of time, we may conclude that innovative companies under these conditions will revert into unbalanced, latent positional/innovative companies.

In our analysis we have assumed that it is the existence of an uncertainty gap between conception and conviction, which initially starts the process of cognitive development and, indirectly, the development of innovative orientation and potential in a company. If this gap disappears we may, according to our previous discussion expect this cognitive process to be reversed, and to lead, instead, to a lower degree of differentiation and cognitive linking. This, then, implies that innovative orientation in the company will tend to disappear, since clear orientation on the company level in our approach demands cognitive clarity on the individual level.

Innovative companies, therefore, according to our discussion will tend to be stable company forms only if their strategic decision makers maintain their uncertainty gaps, and continue actively to collect information on environmental change. If these companies, instead, settle back to enjoy success and give up their active attempts to restructure their view of appropriate company development, they will probably soon lose their clear innovative orientation. This, then, will turn them into latent positional/innovative companies, in which innovative potential is unnecessary, and therefore likely to disappear over time, completing the transition to positional companies. In our empirical example, such a development was as yet hypothetical when the study was completed, since no prolonged success had so far made this type of development applicable. In this respect our discussion therefore is purely theoretical and not backed up by direct empirical data.

With regard to positional companies, on the other hand, success may be expected to reinforce the prevailing orientation and further stabilize the existing mode of company operation. As long as its environment remains stable a positional company will therefore, according to our discussion, be likely to successfully maintain a previously successful way of doing business. This is in contrast to what we have stated above with regard to innovative companies in changeable environments, since success then was viewed as creating a tendency towards a non-appropriate mode of company behaviour. This paradox may explain why many successful innovative companies after some time find it difficult to maintain their positions, even when environmental possibilities remain favourable.

We have now presented our integrated organizational and psychological framework for studying company development. By joining together the company classification model presented in Chapter 3, and the cognitive decision model from this chapter, and attempt has been made to account for variation over time in company development, which cannot be explained by merely employing a traditional economic type of analysis. Cyclical development from one type of company to another, and back again, has been discussed, partly by applying our framework to an empirical situation.

This does not mean that all companies over an extended time period, will go through all phases of the cycle described. This cycle instead shows the possibilities facing a company, but both environmental conditions and strategic decisions will determine if and when a company enters one phase or another.

At the same time it is not implied that a company if it completes a cycle, for instance from positional to innovative and back to positional, will then show the some structure and strategy as initially. Instead it is the general characteristics of the situation which will show up again, summarized by the terms innovative potential and innovative orientation. Many different structures or strategies may lead to the same degree of innovative orientation or potential, and there is no reason why in future cycles specific structures or strategies from earlier cycles will be restored. What will be restored, according to our analysis, is the degree to which these structures and strategies stimulate or inhibit innovation. Similarly each new cycle may be associated with higher or lower results, e.g. profits, and the level of results at any point of time is determined by factors outside our analysis. At the same time the way the company *views* its economic results — as satisfactory or dissatisfactory — is an integral part of the analysis.

Our approach is fundamentally different from the more rational approach to company development, found in the strategic and long range planning literature. In this literature, companies are basically assumed to be able to predict and adequately respond to future environmental conditions of importance to the long run development of a company. They may then plan their strategy and structure to reflect future conditions, and ongoing organizational and psychological mechanisms, which not only adapt to, but also shape environmental conditions, will be of little interest in describing, prescribing and understanding company development. In more complicated development situations — characterized by diversity and genuine uncertainty — such a rational planning approach to company development is severely limited, however, in its applicability. Instead there is a need for an approach which to a greater extent emphasizes that companies not only respond to and predict, but also actively create their future environments.

7.4 Summary of Chapter 7

In this chapter I put forward an integrated psychological and organizational view of company development in changing environments. This view is based on — and constitutes a psychological development of — the company classification model in Chapter 2, in which companies were classified as positional, innovative or latent positional/innovative. In this chapter I try to draw together many of the different aspects of company development discussed in the previous chapters.

For instance, there is a close link with Chapter 4, where we discussed the conditions of company creativity. The cognitive model of decision making suggested in the present chapter can in fact also be used to illustrate the creative process on the individual level, which in this book is seen as crucial to understanding company creativity and innovation.

More generally, this chapter shows how strategy formulation can be considered in an innovative theory of the firm. With the help of the kind of analysis suggested here, differences in strategic development among companies operating in similar environments or over time for given companies an be studied. At the beginning of this book, when we discussed the basic need for an innovative theory of the firm, it was a theory capable of such graduations I had in mind. I hope that the approach developed in this book — and which in a more concentrated form finds expression in this chapter — will be of some use in understanding company development.

At the same time it has been my ambition to provide an analysis which can be applied empirically. For this reason the integrated psychological and organizational discussion of company development in this chapter has been illustrated by a concrete example. The cognitive decision model, furthermore, because of the way it is designed, and because of its links to observable phenomena, may be subjected to more rigorous empirical tests in future research.

CHAPTER 8

General Empirical Indicators of Positional and Innovative Elements in Company Development

8.1 Introduction

In this final chapter a number of empirical indicators of positional and innovative elements in company development will be discussed. This gives a general empirical reference of how the framework may be applied. In this context an analytical distinction will be made between the external and internal environment of a company to facilitate the discussion. The internal environment refers to the organization itself, its structure and resources, while the external environment refers to outside company relationships with customers, suppliers, competitors and so on. This distinction has also been made in our theoretical analysis. While it is difficult to clearly distinguish between internal and external environment of a company, it is necessary to try to do so, if we are to view companies as separate units of analysis.

Traditionally, proponents of organization theory and the economic theory of the firm have used this distinction as a basis for problem specialization. In organization theory the emphasis has been on internal organization, while in economic theory external market conditions have been stressed. Since we are concerned with both the internal and external environment in our analysis, we need to try to combine both these perspectives. In particular we are interested in the interaction between the two which means that we must apply a wide frame of reference in searching for factors which may help to explain company development.

In contrast to our theoretical analysis Chapter 6 and this chapter employs a more variegated and differentiated view of companies as more or less positional or innovative, rather than as examples of the extreme categories. This is natural, since one of the main purposes of theoretical analysis is to concentrate on salient factors, while empirical applications are concerned more with the richness and diversity in real world situations. The stronger the positional or innovative elements are in the internal or external environment — as measured by empirical indicators — the more closely the empirical situations studied will correspond to the ideal, theoretical categories. The purpose of this chapter, then, is to discuss and suggest some general empirical indicators, which may be used for relating empirical data to our theoretical discussion.

The basic idea is that there should be a fit between the external and internal environment of a company (Khandwalla, 1976; Rhenman, 1973). Strong positional elements in the external environment should be matched by strong positional elements in the internal environment, and strong external innovative elements by strong internal innovative elements, to create favourable conditions for company development. At the same time the internal balance in a company between positional and innovative elements will, and should change over time, as we have noted in Chapter 3. In this chapter, however, we will not be concerned with such variation. Instead we will concentrate on the relationships between a company and its external environment.

This view of the need for a matching relationship between the internal and the external environment underlies both the theoretical discussion in previous chapters and the following, more empirically based discussion. The basis for the tentative conclusions in this chapter are empirical work carried out in connection with the present study and other work reported on in the literature. They should be viewed as examples and suggestions, illustrating the possibilities of applying the approach, rather than as definite and comprehensive results.

8.2 Positional elements in external company environments

Positional elements in external company environments may be defined as factors which make it easier for companies to establish and take advantage of strong and lasting environmental relationships. The simpler and more stable the external technological and marketing environment of a company is, the easier it is for the company to obtain and maintain stable relationships with its external environment. Consequently, the stronger the positional elements in the external environment of the company then are.

Slow and continuous, rather than rapid and discontinuous, technological change is one major positional element in external company environments. For instance, technological advances in mature technologies, such as electronics, usually are more gradual from the point of view of companies working in the area, than advances in new technology areas, such as laser techniques. The overall research environments of companies working in mature areas of technology will, from a technological point of view, therefore usually be more positional in nature, than the research environments of companies working in new areas of technology.

To companies who are technologically leading in new areas of technology (Jewkes, Sawers and Stillerman, 1958, Langrisch and coworkers, 1972), outside research may, however, be a relatively positional element in the company's external environment if it is line with, or already has been anticipated, by the company's own research.

Stability in the external technological environment of a company may therefore be achieved by technological leadership, or by the company working in product areas, where technological change for the industry as a whole has slowed down. Examples of the former are synthetic fibres and copying machines, where for long periods of time Du Pont and Xerox have held, and been able to exploit, and established technological leadership position. Examples of the latter are many capital goods, such as TV, radio and car batteries. In these areas technological development has been slow for many years, and radical changes in technology have not characterized the situation.

If a company has a technological leadership position protected by strong patents (Taylor and Silberston, 1973; Silberston, 1975), the positional element will probably be stronger in most cases, than if its technological advantage is only due to its general technological competence and unpatentable know-how. In radically new product and technology areas patent protection is usually easier to achieve, than in more established areas. This leads to the paradox, that positional elements with regard to technology may well be stronger in new areas, than in more established ones.

Stability in the external marketing environment of a company may — as we have discussed more fully in Chapter 5 — be due to stable buyer preferences and/or defensive marketing practices. In a static perspective a company may choose product differentiation or market segmentation to achieve a more stable market. In a dynamic perspective — which is emphasized in this book — they may try to stabilize their market relationships by employing a more closed and restricted, rather than a more open and flexible marketing strategy. For this purpose selective marketing techniques, such as personal selling and direct advertising, are better suited than non-selective marketing techniques, such as mass advertising.

A special type of defensive marketing involves implicit or explicit oligopolistic cooperation between competitors (Fellner, 1949). Such collusion will tend to stabilize the marketing situations of competing companies, both in the short and long run, but may also lead to undesirable consequences for society as a whole.

The question whether limitations on competition — oligopoly or monopoly—impede or stimulate company innovation is highly controversial (Scherer, 1970). Schumpter (1942) claimed that monopoly conditions are favourable to innovation, by creating greater resources for research and development, and a similar argument may be put forward with regard to oligopoly situations.

This view has, however, been challenged by many writers. With regard to our analysis we may argue that active competition creates a greater need for innovation, if companies are to survive. Competition will not, however, automatically lead to either greater innovative potential or a clear innovative orientation, which in our approach are crucial to company innovation. We thus need a broader framework — including also organizational and psychological factors — in order to analyse the effects of competition on company innovation.

8.3 Innovative elements in external company environments

Innovative elements in external company environments may be defined as factors which make it necessary for companies to often and radically change their strategy and structure, to achieve satisfactory environmental relationships.

The more complex and unstable the external technological and marketing environment of a company is, the more it is characterized by innovative elements. As in the case of positional elements in the external environment of a company, a distinction is thus made between the internal and external environment of a company.

With regard to external technological environment, rapid idea generation and methodological development in an area are important innovative elements. The general implications of new technology for companies within an industry will depend, however, on the extent to which individual companies can keep secret, patent or otherwise protect their new ideas. The wider and more rapid the spread of new ideas (Gerstenfeld, 1976), and the more difficult it is to protect these ideas, the stronger the innovative elements are likely to be, for the companies concerned.

Innovative elements may also be expected to increase in importance if research is published and the results made generally available, for instance in the scientific press or in trade journals. Also, the use of licensing agreements (Taylor and Silberston, 1973), or other means for technology transfer between companies will probably tend to increase the innovative elements in the technological environments of companies working in an area. Possible empirical indicators of these innovative elements in a technological environment are the number of relevant books or articles published, the number of scientific conferences held and the number and extent of license agreements.

With regard to external marketing environments we have already discussed the role of competition in promoting innovation. An increase in competition may generally be assumed to add to the innovative elements in a marketing environment, but not necessarily increase the rate of innovation for an individual company. A company may not want to, or be able to, respond to a need for innovation by innovating. If it does not respond adequately, it will, however, sooner or later experience difficulties in company development.

Possible empirical indicators of an increase in competition may be found in the economic literature (Scherer, 1970; Parker, 1974). One such indicator is the number of actual competitors. Competition in the marketing environment of a company may then be viewed as increasing with the number of competitors. This number may increase as a result either of the company's own action, e.g. when a company goes international, or as a result of new competitors entering its existing market. Another possible indicator is the use of active means of competition, for instance price; increased use of which may be seen as reflecting — and leading to — increased competition.

The willingness of buyers to accept new products, and how rapidly they do this (Rasmussen, 1955), will also influence the extent to which innovative elements characterize the external marketing environment of a company. The more willing buyers are to accepts new products — and the sooner they may be persuaded to do so — the stronger the innovative tendencies in the market will be. Among other things, this will influence the length of time and amount of marketing effort necessary to launch a new product.

The more rapidly a new product can gain market acceptance, the quicker the company thus can achieve a change in innovative orientation — based on its selling radically new products — and the lower the cost of achieving this change in strategy. In the case of long acceptance periods for new products, innovative elements deriving from rapid technological change will be counteracted by the slower process of product introduction on the market. A typical example of this is the pharmaceutical industry (Skagius, 1968), where long market introduction periods greatly slow down the marketing of new products. In this case relatively strong positional elements in the external marketing environment, work against the utilization by companies of relatively strong innovative elements in the external technological environment.

8.4 Positional elements in internal company environments

Positional elements in the internal environment of a company are factors within the company, which make it easier to take advantage of positional elements in the external environment. Such factors depend on the structure and strategy of the company that is its internal resources and how they are used to promote stability.

With regard to technical resources, designing these to gain specialization and large scale advantages in producing and marketing existing products, may be seen as a strong positional element in the internal environment of a company. This type of resource allocation may be achieved, for instance, by investing in specialized machinery with high fixed costs, but low costs per produced unit at high levels of capacity utilization. Or by vertical integration (Mattsson, 1969), for instance when a manufacturer uses its own sales force, rather than agents, in selling abroad.

Such measures may be expected to lead to increased efficiency and lower costs, if companies can plan for and realize a sufficiently high and stable level of production and sales. But at the same time they will usually lead to inflexibility, with regard to product and marketing strategy. Product innovation will become difficult, both because of the specialized nature of existing production facilities and because of difficulties in reaching new customer groups.

Economic effects of this type are dealt with in most books and courses teaching business administration, but usually in a static perspective, emphasizing the advantages of this type of positional element, for carrying out the existing line of business. Little attention is usually paid to the possible negative effects of such measures for long run company development, by inhibiting innovation.

With regard to organization structure, a highly formalized, bureaucratic type organization may, as we have discussed more fully in Chapter 3, be viewed as a strong positional element in the internal environment of a company. This is particularly the case since such organizations may be expected to lead to organizational inflexibility. Not only will organization members be constrained from carrying out change by the prevailing rules and regulations. Their ability and willingness to initiate and carry out change will probably also be negatively effected by this type of organization structure. Changing the structure to make it more flexible, will then have little effect on the innovative potential of the company, if organization members have not been able to develop their creative capacity.

Possible empirical indicators of a formalized bureaucratic structure have been suggested by many organization analysts. We may for instance look at how closely specified jobs are (Aiken and Hage, 1973), or the extent to which planning and budgeting procedures are regulated in detail in organization manuals (Samuelson, 1973). The more numerous and specific these specifications are, and the less deviation is accepted, the higher the degree of formalization is, and the lower the organization's flexibility to respond to unexpected change.

In our approach, as we have seen in Chapters 4 and 7, strategy is basically related to how leading decision makers view company development. In this connection we may distinguish between *internal orientation*, when decision makers emphasize elements in their internal environment, and *external orientation*, when they give greater weight to elements in the external environment. Internal orientation on the part of strategic decision makers may then be regarded as a basically positional element in the internal environment of a company. Company characteristics, rather than outside conditions, are in this case the focus of interest. This should tend to lead to a greater concern for producing and marketing existing products, than for developing new ones. The decision maker, in other words, then is better informed with regard to what the company can do, than what it should do, in order to respond to changes in its external environment.

It should be possible to use variables relating to both the experience and education of individual decision makers and overall company strategy as empirical indicators of internal and external orientation. The longer an individual has been working in a particular company, for instance, the greater his knowledge and experience of this company's internal functioning should be. Consequently, the greater his tendency also should be to give priority to solving internal problems, rather than to responding to external opportunities. If he has been highly specialized in his line of work this tendency should be stronger since assessing external opportunities for company development requires a broad knowledge of company potential.

With regard to education, higher formal education (Blau and Scott, 1963) may be expected to contribute to a more external orientation, by leading to a more cosmopolitan, rather than local, value structure (Merton, 1957; Gouldner, 1957) and a wider, more general knowledge of society. Professionals, then, with academic training and credentials, should tend to be more externally oriented than decision makers with more internal, company-based training. But even among professionals we may well find differences in this respect (Friedlander, 1971). Technical training, by being most applicable to analysing internal technical conditions may for instance lead to a more internal orientation among company decision makers, than training in marketing, which deals more with external relationships.

In addition to the above type of empirical indicators of internal–external orientation, based on the characteristics of individual decision makers, we may also use indicators more directly related to company strategy, as we have seen in Chapter 6. Following our theoretical discussion we may use these indicators to study how consistently function is related to performance, and to compare companies with regard to how well they conform to our theoretical categories.

In accordance with our previous discussion in this book, companies with strong positional elements in their internal and external environments may be expected to emphasize cost reduction measures more than new product development, and to be more concerned with product modification, than product innovation. At any given point of time they will, therefore, probably have a relatively high proportion of old and established, rather than radically new products in their assortments. This, then, means that they will be more product oriented, that is interested in producing and selling existing products, than market oriented, that is concerned with satisfying unfulfilled buyer needs, by developing new products. Their marketing strategies, as a consequence, should be more closed and restricted, rather than open and flexible, and they should tend to employ selective, rather than non-selective marketing techniques to achieve their goals.

In summary, positional companies depend on stable environmental conditions for success, and will themselves have a stabilizing influence on general economic conditions for society as a whole. Their sales and profits are likely to be relatively stable over time, as long as their outside conditions remain stable. Up until recently such stagnation on the company and societal level has generally been regarded as a threat to economic welfare. Today, however, necessary and desirable restrictions on economic growth (Mishan, 1969) are being more and more emphasized in the political and economic debate. Economic stagnation may then be viewed as an asset, rather than as a liability to society, and in this connection positional companies take on added interest as possible means for achieving and maintaining stability and minimal growth.

8.5 Innovative elements in internal company environments

Innovative elements in the internal environment of a company are factors within the company, which make it easier for the company to respond to and initiate innovative change. As with regard to positional elements we may distinguish between factors related to the structure and the strategy of a company.

With regard to structure, flexibility in production and marketing are of course important innovative elements. Increased flexibility in production may be achieved, for instance, by a company subcontracting the manufacturing of components to other companies. Car manufacturing companies, for example, often use this production strategy. Flexibility in marketing, on the other hand, may be achieved by making less specialized products and selling these through many different channels of distribution. Mass marketing of consumer goods usually is based on creating and utilizing this type of marketing situations. The greater their production and marketing flexibility is, the easier it should be for a company to find new products compatible with their existing facilities.

With regard to the internal organization of a company, a relatively un-formalized and loosely coupled structure — for instance a matrix organization — may be viewed as an innovative element. This type of structure, as we have seen in Chapter 3, tends to lead to high organizational flexibility and diversity, which together imply favorable conditions for company creativity and innovation, as we have discussed more fully in Chapter 4.

With regard to empirical indicators of innovative elements in the internal organization we may use the same measures as we have discussed with regard to positional elements, but with opposite values.

Relatively unspecified jobs and open and flexible planning and budgeting procedures, as well as external orientation on the part of decision makers, may therefore be employed as empirical indicators of innovative elements in the internal organization of a company. As in the case of positional tendencies both the experience and education of individual decision makers and factors related to overall company strategy may be used as indicators of external orientation. Outside company experience and education — for instance professional training and work in other types of organizations — may be expected to lead to greater external orientation. It is also likely that market-directed thinking will lead to a more external orientation for a company decision maker, than techno-logically directed thinking. These hypotheses are the reverse of what we noted in the previous section with regard to positional elements.

With regard to empirical indicators of appropriate company performance, when strong innovative elements characterize internal and external environ-ments, it is again a question of applying our theoretical framework. Highly innovative companies may be expected to have a relatively high proportion radically new products, at any point of time, and a relatively low proportion established products or product modifications. They may be expected to emphasize research and development more than cost reductions. Their marketing strategies as a result will need to be open and flexible rather than closed and restricted, and their marketing techniques non-specific, rather than specific.

In other words innovative companies not only will utilize, but also will tend to create instability and change, in their external environments. Their sales and profits are likely to develop unevenly over time and to show clear cyclical trends.

This, then, will be due not only to external economic conditions, but also to company policy. When many new products are being developed investment will be high and sales and profits low, and when and if they are successfully introduced on the market, sales and profits will go up. If this type of company development, and its implications for overall economic development, is desirable or not from a societal point of view is a political question, which cannot be answered by our analysis. The great present day need in many companies for innovation and creativity is clear, however, and cannot be ignored, least of all by the companies involved.

8.6 Summary of Chapter 8

In this chapter I discuss some possible general empirical indicators of positional and innovative elements in the company's external and internal environment. The main purpose here has been to exemplify various factors important to our theory, in order to illustrate the possibility of empirical testing. In Chapter 6 more specific empirical indicators were discussed, in the context of company R and D strategies.

In the external environment, technological and market development — which companies can to some extent influence within their own spheres — are probably the major mutually dependent determinants of company behaviour, and are emphasized both in Chapter 6 and this chapter.

Examples of positional elements in the external environment are certain technological and market factors — patents and product differentiation for example — which create varying states of monopoly. Examples of innovative elements in the technological environment could be a high rate of technological development and a relatively high level of exchange of research results between and within companies. On the marketing side a major innovative element could be active and relatively intense competition between companies. Unstable customer preferences may be expected to reinforce this innovative element, while stable customer preferences represent a positional element.

In the company's internal environment a striving for advantages of scale and specialization generally may be assumed to suggest an inflexible resource structure, and thus represents a positional element in the company's internal environment. While a flexible resource structure, perhaps as a result of high technological and product substitutability, can represent an innovative element in the company's internal environment.

As regards organization structure, a high degree of formalization can be taken to represent a positional element, and a low degree of formalization an innovative element.

In planning, and budget routines and job descriptions, for example, a high degree of formalization could express itself in a multiplicity of long run detailed plans and budgets, and in an inclination towards very specific and clearly defined job descriptions. Short term general plans and budgets, together with more generalized and non-specific job descriptions, on the other hand, could reflect a lower degree of formalization.

In the company's control system the degree of internal or external orientation of the management members has been suggested as an empirical indicator of positional or innovative tendencies. By internal orientation I mean here that factors in the company's internal environment are the chief consideration in decision making, while by external orientation I mean that factors linked to the external environment are given greater weight. Possible empirical indicators of

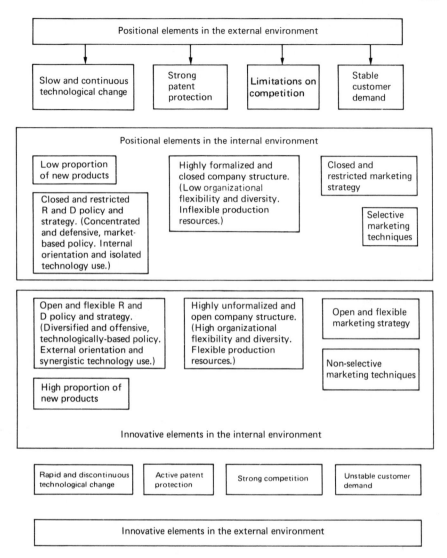

Figure 8.1. Innovative and positional elements in the Internal and External Environment of a Company.

the type of orientation may be the kind of experience and training represented by company members and the strength of the technologically of market-directed thinking.

Long experience and job specialization in one particular company, a low level of formal education and technologically-directed thinking can reflect an internal orientation, while experience from many companies and types of job, a high level of formal training (academic training for example) and market-directed thinking can reflect an external orientation.

In Chapter 6 indicators of internal or external orientation more directly related to overall company strategy were discussed in the context of R and D strategies.

With regard to performance company activities can reflect the existence of strong positional and innovative elements in the external and internal environments, for instance in the development of new products or in sales and profit trends. Thus we can expect that the proportion of radically new products will be greater and the proportion of product modifications lower in innovative companies than in positional companies. Furthermore positional companies will probably have more closed and restricted marketing strategies — and selective marketing techniques — while innovative companies will probably have a more open and flexible strategies and employ non-selective techniques.

Finally, sales and profits are likely to develop more evenly in positional companies than in innovative companies, because both the product supply and customers' demands are more stable. Sales and profit trends in innovative companies are likely to display clear cyclical trends (even if the long run trend is positive) because of the switches in investments between new and established products and between different stages in the development and marketing of individual products.

In this discussion I have been assuming a basic fit between the internal and external environments of the respective companies. In Figure 8.1 I have summarized the factors in the external and internal environment which I have suggested in this chapter as the distinguishing features of the positional and innovative company and of the external environmental conditions best suited to the two types of companies.

References

Aaker, D. A., 1971, *Multivariate Analysis in Marketing: Theory and Application*, Belmont Calif.: Wadsworth.

Achilladeles, B., Jervis, P., and Robertson, A., 1971, *Report on Project SAPPHO to the Science Research Council: A Study of Success and Failure in Innovation*, Sussex, England: Science Policy Research Unit, University of Sussex.

Aiken, M., and Hage, J., 1973, 'Organizational Interdependence and Intra-organizational Structure'. In W. V. Heydebrand (Ed.), *Comparative Organizations*, 269–294, Englewood Cliffs, N.J: Prentice Hall.

Albrow, M., 1970, *Bureaucracy*, London: Praeger.

Anderson, H. H. (Ed.), 1959, *Creativity and its Cultivation*, New York: Harper and Row.

Ansoff, H. I., 1965, *Corporate Strategy*, New York: McGraw-Hill.

Arndt, J., 1974, *Market Segmentation*, Bergen: Universitetsförlaget.

Arpi, B., 1970, 'MIS, MARKIS och framtidens marknadsföringsfunktion', *Marknadsvetande*, **1**, 5–18.

Ashby, W. R., 1960, *Design for a Brain*, London: Chapman and Hall.

Back, R., 1973, *Beslutskoordinering*, Stockholm: Economic Research Institute at the Stockholm School of Economics.

Bannister, D., and Fransella, F., 1971, *Inquiring Man. The Theory of Personal Constructs*, Middlesex, England: Penguin.

Barron, F., 1955, 'The Disposition towards Originality', *Journal of Abnormal and Social Psychology*, **51**, 478–485.

Becker, S., and Whisler, T. L., 1967, 'The Innovative Organization: A Selective View of Current Theory and Research', *The Journal of Business*, **40**, No. 4, 462–469.

Bell, G., 1967, 'Formality versus Flexibility in Complex Organizations'. In G. Bell (Ed.), *Organizations and Human Behavior*, 97–106, Englewood Cliffs, N.J.: Prentice–Hall.

Bieri, J., Atkins, A. L., Briar, S., Lobeck, R., Miller, H., and Tripodi, T., 1966, *Clinical and Social Judgement*, New York: Wiley.

Blau, P. M., and Scott, W. R., 1963, *Formal Organizations*, London: Routledge and Keagan Paul.

Bolton, N., 1972, *The Psychology of Thinking*, London: Methuen.

Boulding, K. E., 1966, 'The Economics of Knowledge and the Knowledge of Economics', *American Economic Review*, **56**, 1–13.

Bruner, J. S., 1965, 'Some Observations on Effective Cognitive Processes'. In G. A. Steiner (Ed.), *The Creative Organization*, 106–117, Chicago: University of Chicago Press.

Buckley, W., 1967, *Sociology and Modern Systems Theory*, Englewood Cliffs, N.J.: Prentice–Hall.

Burns, T., and Stalker, G. M., 1961, *The Management of Innovation*, London: Tavistock.

Carlson, S., 1973, 'Investments in Knowledge and the Cost of Information', *Annales Academicas Regiae Scientarium*, 15–28, Uppsala.

114

Chamberlin, E. H., 1933, *The Theory of Monopolistic Competition*, Cambridge, Mass.: Harvard University Press.
Chandler, A. D., 1962, *Strategy and Structure*, Cambridge, Mass.: MIT Press.
Cropley, A. J., 1967, *Creativity*, London: Longmans.
Crosby, A., 1968, *Creativity and Performance in Industrial Organization*, London: Tavistock.
Crozier, M., 1964, *The Bureaucratic Phenomenon*, London: Tavistock.
Cyert, R. M., and March, J. G., 1963, *A Behavioral Theory of the Firm*, Englewodd Cliffs, N.J.: Prentice-Hall.
Dreistadt, R., 1969, 'The Use of Analogies and Incubation in Obtaining Insights in Creative Problem Solving', *Journal of Psychology*, 71, 159–175.
Ehrenzweig, A., 1967, *The Hidden Order of Art: A Study in the Psychology of Artistic Imagination*, Berkeley, Calif.: University of California Press.
Fayol, H., 1949, *General and Industrial Management*, London: Pitmans.
Fellner, W., 1949, *Competition Among the Few*, New York: Knopf.
Festinger, L., 1957, *A Theory of Cognitive Dissonance*, Evanston, Ill.: Row–Peterson.
Freeman, C., 1974, *The Economics of Industrial Innovation*, Middlesex, England: Penguin.
Friedlander, F., 1971, 'Performance and Orientation Structures of Research Scientists', *Organizational Behavior and Human Performance*, 6, 169–183.
Fulgosi, A., and Guilford, J. P., 1968, 'Short term Incubation in Divergent Production', *American Journal of Psychology*, 81, 241–246.
Galbraith, J., 1973, *Designing Complex Organizations*, Reading, Mass. : Addison-Wesley.
Gardner, R. W., and Schoen, R. A., 1962, 'Differentiation and Abstraction in Concept Formation', *Psychological Monographs*, 76, No 41.
Gerstenfeld, A., 1976, 'Interdependence and Innovation', *Omega*, 5, 35–41.
Glaser, B., and Strauss, A., 1967, *The Discovery of Grounded Theory: Strategies for Qualitative Research*, Chicago: Aldine.
Gold, B., 1975, 'Alternative Strategies for Advancing a Company's Technology', *Research Management*, 18, 24–29.
Gouldner, A. W., 1954, *Patterns of Industrial Bureaucracy*, Glencoe, Ill.: Free Press.
Gouldner, A. W., 1957, 'Cosmopolitans and Locals: Towards an Analysis of lantent Social Roles', *Administrative Science Quarterly*, 2, 281–306.
Grinyer, P. H., 1971, 'The Anatomy of Business Strategic Planning Reconsidered', *Journal of Management Studies*, 8, No 2, 199–212.
Hage, J., and Aiken, M., 1970, *Social Change in Complex Organizations*, New York: Random House.
Hedberg, B. T., Nyström, P. C., and Starbuck, W. H., 1976, 'Camping on Seesaws: Prescriptions for a Self-designing Organization', *Administrative Science Quarterly*, 21, 41–65.
Henderson, J. M., and Quandt, R. E., 1958, *Microeconomic Theory. A Mathematical Approach*, New York: McGraw-Hill.
Hill, R. M., and Hlavacek, J. D., 1972, 'The Venture Team: A New Concept in Marketing Organization', *Journal of Marketing*, 36, 44–50.
Hoffman, L. R., 1969, 'Homogeneity of Member Personality and its Effect on Group Problem Solving', *Journal of Abnormal Social Psychology*, 58, 27–32.
Horvath, D., 1976, *Kriterier och principer för företagsorganisation*, Lund: Studentlitteratur.
Jewkes, J., Sawers, D., and Stillerman, R., 1958, *The Sources of Invention*, London: Macmillan.
Johansson, J., 1976, *Styrelsearbetets marknadsorientering i svenska företag*, Uppsala: Företagsekonomiska institutionen vid Uppsala universitet.
Jönsson, S. A., 1973, *Decentralisering och utveckling*, Göteborg: BAS.

Khandwalla, P. N., 1976, 'The Techno-economic Ecology of Corporate Strategy', *Journal of Management Studies*, February, 62–75.

Kingdon, D. R., 1973, *Matrix Organization: Managing Information Technologies*, London: Tavistock.

Knight, K., 1976, 'Matrix Organization: A Review', *Journal of Management Studies*, 13, 111–130.

Koestler, A., 1964, *The Act of Creation*, London: Hutchinson.

Kotler, P., 1967, *Marketing Management*, Englewood Cliffs, N.J.: Prentice–Hall.

Krech, D., Crutchfield, R. S., and Ballachey, E. L., 1962, *Individual in Society*, New York: McGraw-Hill.

Lamberton, D. M. (Ed.), 1971, *Economics of Information and Knowledge*, Middlesex, England: Penguin.

Langrisch, J., Gibbons, M., Evans, W. G., and Jevons, F. R., 1972, *Wealth from Knowledge*, London: Macmillan.

Lawrence, P. R., and Lorsch, J. W., 1967, *Organization and Environment*, Boston: Harvard University Press.

McKenney, J. L., and Keen, P. G. W., 1974, 'How Managers' Minds Work', *Harvard Business Review*, May–June, 79–90.

Mansfield, E., 1968, *The Economics of Technological Change*, London: Longmans.

March, J. G., 1976, 'The Technology of Foolishness'. In J. G. March and J. P. Olsen, *Ambiguity and Choice in Organizations*, 69–81. Bergen: Universitetsförlaget.

March, J. G., and Olsen, J. P., 1976, *Ambiguity and Choice in Organizations*, Bergen: Universitetsförlaget.

March, J. G., and Simon, H. A., 1958, *Organizations*, New York: Wiley.

Marquis, D., and Myers, S., 1969, *Successful Industrial Innovations*, Washington: National Science Foundation.

Mathiesen, H. H., 1971, 'Produktdifferentiering og markedssegmentering som alternative marknadsföringsstrategier', *Marknadsvetande*, 2, 24–28.

Mattsson, L. G., 1969, *Integration and Efficiency in Marketing Systems*, Stockholm: The Economic Research Institute at the Stockholm School of Economics.

May, R., 1959, 'The Nature of Creativity'. In H. H. Andersson (Ed.), *The Cultivation of Creativity*, 55–68, New York: Harper and Row.

Meadow, A., Parnes, S. J., and Reese, M., 1959, 'Influence of Brain Storming Instructions and Problems Sequence on a Creative Problem-solving Test', *Journal of Applied Psychology*, 43, 413–416.

Merton, R. K., 1940, 'Bureaucratic Structure and Personality', *Social Forces*, 18, 560–568.

Merton, R. K., 1957, *Social Theory and Social Structure*, New York: The Free Press.

Miller, G. A., 1967, 'The Magical Number Seven, Plus or Minus Two: Some Limits on our Capacity for Processing Information'. In M. Alexis and C. Wilson (Eds.), *Organizational Decision Making*, Englewood Cliffs, N.J.: Prentice–Hall.

Mintzberg, H., 1973a., *The Nature of Managerial Work*, New York: Harper and Row.

Mintzberg, H., 1973b, 'Strategy-making in Three Modes', *California Management Review*, 16, 44–53.

Mintzberg, H., Raisinghani, D., and Théorêt, A., 1976, 'The Structure of "Unstructured Decision Processes"', *Administrative Science Quarterly*, 21, 246–275.

Mishan, E. J., 1969, *The Costs of Economic Growth*, Middlesex, England: Penguin.

Montgomery, D. B., and Urban, G. L., 1970, *Applications of Management Science to Marketing*, Englewood Cliffs, N.J.: Prentice–Hall.

Mumford, E., and Pettigrew, A., 1975, *Implementing Strategic Decisions*, London: Longman.

Näslund, B., and Sellstedt, B. 1973, 'A Note on the Implementation and Use of Models for R and D Planning', *Research Policy*, 2, 72–85.

Naylor, T. H., Balintfy, J. L., Burdick, D. S., and Chu, K., 1966, *Computer Simulation Techniques*, New York: Wiley.

Norman, R., 1971, 'Organizational Innovativeness: Product Variation and Reorientation', *Administrative Science Quarterly*, **16**, 203–215.

Nyström, H., 1970, *Retail Pricing*, Stockholm: Economic Research Institute at the Stockholm School of Economics.

Nyström, H., 1971, 'Bara effektiv eller innovativ', *Ekonomen*, **4**, 17–28.

Nyström, H., 1972a, 'Statiska och dynamiska marknadsföringsstrategier', *Marknadsvetande*, **1**, 21–35.

Nyström, H., 1972b, 'Marknadsosäkerhet och marknadsbeslut', *Marknadsvetande*, **4**, 26–33.

Nyström, H., 1974, 'Uncertainty, Information and Organizational Decision-making', *Swedish Journal of Economics*, **76**, 131–139.

Nyström, H., 1977, *Company Strategies for Research and Development*, Uppsala: The Swedish University of Agricultural Sciences.

Osborn, A. F., 1953, *Applied Imagination*, New York: Scribners.

Parker, J. E. S., 1974, *The Economics of Innovation*, London: Longman.

Parnes, S. J., and Meadow, A., 1959, 'Effects of "Brainstorming" Instructions on Creative Problem Solving by Trained and Untrained Subjects', *Journal of Educational Psychology*, **50**, 171–176.

Peters, J. T., and Hammond, K. R., 1974, 'A Note on Intuitive vs Analytical Thinking', *Organizational Behaviour and Human Performance*, **12**, 125–131.

Poincaré, H., 1913, *The Foundations of Science*. New York: Science Press.

Pugh, D. S., Hickson, D. J., Hinings, C. R., and Turner, C., 1968, 'Dimensions of Organization Structure', *Administrative Science Quarterly*, **13**, 65–106.

Rasmussen, A., 1955, *Pristeori eller parameterteori*, Köpenhamn: Ehrvervsøkonomisk Förlag.

Raven, B. H., and Rietsema, J. R., 1957, 'The Effects of Varied Clarity of Group Goal and Group Path Upon the Individual and his Relation to his Group', *Human Relations*, **10**, 29–45.

Rhenman, E., Strömberg, L., and Westerberg, G., 1963, *Om linje och stab. En studie av konflikt och samverkan*. Stockholm: Economic Research Institute at the Stockholm School of Economics.

Rhenman, E., 1973, *Organization Theory for Long Range Planning*, London: Wiley.

Roberts, E. B., 1976, 'Technology Strategy for the Medium-size Company', *Research Management*, **19**, 29–32.

Roe, A., 1952, *The Making of a Scientist*, New York: Dodd Mead.

Rokeach, M., 1960, *The Open and Closed Mind*, New York: Basic Books.

Rogers, C. R., 1959, 'Towards a Theory of Creativity'. In H. H. Andersson (Ed.), *Creativity and its Cultivation*, 69–82, New York: Harper and Row.

Rothwell, R., 1975, 'From Invention to New Business via the New Venture Approach, *Management Decision*, **13**, No 1, 10–21.

Samuelson, L., 1973, *Effektiv budgetering*, Stockholm: Economic Research Institute of the Stockholm School of Economics.

Sandkull, B. 1970, *Innovative Behaviour of Organizations. The Case of New Products*, Lund: Studentlitteratur.

Scherer, F. M., 1970, *Industrial Market Structure and Economic Performance*, Chicago: Rand McNally.

Schroder, H. M., Driver, M. J., and Streufert, S., 1967, *Human Information Processing*, New York: Holt, Rinehart and Winston.

Schumpeter, J., 1934, *The Theory of Economic Development*, Cambridge, Mass.: Harvard University Press.

Schumpeter, J., 1942, *Capitalism, Socialism and Democracy*, New York: Harper and Row.

Scott, W. A., 1963, 'Conceptualizing and Measuring Structural Properties of Cognition'. In O. J. Harvey (Ed.), *Motivation and Social Interaction: Cognitive Determinants*, New York: Ronald Press.

Selznick, P., 1949, *TVA and the Grass Roots*, Berkeley and Los Angeles: University of California Press.

Shackle, G. L. S., 1958, *Time in Economics*, Amsterdam: North-Holland.

Shouksmith, G., 1970, *Intelligence, Creativity and Cognitive Style*, New York: Wiley.

Silberston, A., 1975, 'Impact of the Patent System on the Creation and Diffusion of New Technology', *Omega*, **3**, 9–22.

Skagius, K., 1968, 'R and D Policy in a Swedish Pharmaceutical Company', *Journal of Scientific Technical Research*, **3**, 92–99.

Smith, W. R., 1956, 'Product Differentiation and Market Segmentation as Alternative Marketing Strategies', *Journal of Marketing*, **21**, 3–8.

Steiner, G. A. (Ed.), 1965, *The Creative Organization*, Chicago: University of Chicago Press.

Tayor, C. T., and Silberston, Z. A., 1973, *The Economic Impact of the Patent System*, London: Cambridge University Press.

Taylor, C. W., and Barron, F. (Eds.), 1963, *Scientific Creativity*, New York: Wiley.

Taylor, F. W., 1911, *The Principles of Scientific Management*, New York: Harper and Row.

Thompson, V. A., 1961, *Modern Organization*, New York: Knopf.

Thompson, V. A., 1969, *Bureaucracy and Innovation*, University, Alabama: University of Alabama Press.

Vernon, P. E., (Ed.), 1970, *Creativity*, Middlesex, England: Penguin.

Walker, A. H., and Lorsch, J. W., 1970, *Studies in Organization Design*, Homewood, Ill.: Irwin–Dorsey.

Wallach, M. A., and Kogan, N., 1965, 'A New Look at the Creativity — Intelligence Distinction', *Journal of Personality*, **3**, 348–369.

Wallas, G., 1926, *The Art of Thought*, New York: Harcourt Brace.

Weber, M., 1947, *Theory of Social and Economic Organization*, New York: The Free Press.

Wertheimer, M., 1959, *Productive Thinking*, New York: Harper and Row.

Wilson, J. Q., 1966, 'Innovation in Organization: Notes towards a Theory', In V. H. Vroom (Ed.), *Organizational Design and Research*, Pittsburgh: University of Pittsburgh Press.

Wren, D. A., 1972, *The Evolution of Management Thought*, New York: Ronald Press.

Index

122

124